P9-BZR-087

CRAFTS AND KEEPSAKES
FOR THE HOLIDAYS

Christmas with Martha Stewart Living

CRAFTS AND KEEPSAKES
FOR THE HOLIDAYS

Clarkson Potter/Publishers
New York

Copyright © 1999 Martha Stewart Living
Omnimedia LLC, 20 West 43rd Street,
New York, NY 10036

All rights reserved. No part of this book
may be reproduced in any form or by any
means without the prior written permission
of the publisher.

Originally published in book form by
Martha Stewart Living Omnimedia LLC
in 1999.
Published simultaneously by Clarkson
Potter, Oxmoor House, Inc.,
and Leisure Arts.

A portion of this work was previously
published in MARTHA STEWART LIVING.

Published by Clarkson Potter,
201 East 50th Street, New York,
NY 10022.

Member of the Crown Publishing Group.
Random House, Inc. New York, Toronto,
London, Sydney, Auckland
http://www.randomhouse.com
Clarkson Potter, Potter, and colophon
are trademarks of Random House, Inc.

Printed in the United States of America.

Executive Editor: Kathleen Hackett
Art Director: Linda Kocur
Text by Terri Trucco
with David Nussbaum
Assistant Art Director: Jill Groeber

Library of Congress Cataloging in
Publication Data is available upon request.
ISBN: 0-609-80440-5 (alk. paper)

10 9 8 7 6 5 4 3 2 1
First Edition

CONTENTS

INTRODUCTION

It has been a real pleasure for me watching this book evolve from an idea to reality. The "homemade," the "handcrafted," the "heirloom," and the "keepsake" have always been for me the real essence of the holiday season. I personally would rather receive something fashioned by hand than anything store-bought, and I have always tried to give presents to my loved ones that I have made myself. ✳ My tradition of homemade gifts goes all the way back to my childhood, when cookie and cake baking were essential to celebrating the holidays in our home. We packaged noel nut balls, Vienna tarts, and springerle cookies in hand-painted tins, and wrapped Mrs. Maus's fruitcakes in cellophane with colorful ribbons. I knitted scarves and mittens for my brothers and sisters, and one year I spent nine months knitting a very special herringbone scarf for my father. I even recall knitting argyle socks—in the most difficult pattern—for a friend! ✳ When I got married I started a "plum pudding" tradition, steaming dozens and dozens of puddings in specially designed handmade bowls. I still make them—only fewer, because the tradition had gotten out of hand. But no one has forgotten the fragrant pudding with the handwritten labels and the recipe for brandied hard sauce. I have also baked hundreds of panettone in brown-paper sacks, giant sugar cookies, and shortbreads to give as gifts. ✳ In addition to the baked goods, I have found myself creating more craft gifts. One year I made silk-velvet scarves for my women friends and silk-lined fine-woolen mufflers for the men in my life. Just this past year I sewed several dozen stockings from remnants of antique ingrain carpeting. I got a lot of pleasure from making these gifts, and the enthusiasm with which they were received made me start thinking right away of the following year's presents. ✳ In this book we have assembled so many wonderful projects that have lasting and memorable qualities. The entire editorial staff of MARTHA STEWART LIVING contributed to the creation of these ideas, and we are proud to take you through all of them, step by step, so that your personal gifts will be successful and gratifying, not only to receive, but to make.

Martha Stewart

part 1

KEEPSAKES FOR EVERY CHRISTMAS

THE FIRST YEAR, IT'S A NEW GIFT, ALL SPARKLE AND SURPRISE. BUT A STAR, A STOCKING, OR A WREATH— ONE YOU HAVE MADE—WILL BE UNWRAPPED AND EXCLAIMED OVER THE NEXT YEAR AND THE NEXT, FOR HOLIDAYS TO COME. HUNG AND HANDLED LOVINGLY, IT BECOMES A WELCOME SIGN OF THE SEASON, AS ITS SPARKLE SOFTENS TO THE LUSTER OF A FAMILY TRADITION.

STOCKINGS
AND
TINY
PRESENTS

Nothing expresses the innocent hope and instinctive generosity of the holidays more than a Christmas stocking. And there is no more fitting gift, for anyone you truly care about, than a stocking you have made yourself. It is not only a charming creation from your own hands, but

an invitation to participate joyfully in the great tradition of giving. For the Christmas connoisseur, stockings like the ones in this chapter will be the pride of the season, happily displayed to all. ✳ We don't know exactly where and when stockings were first hung, but the practice is part of a varied and magical set of Christmas customs. In many places in Europe and in

Latin America, children set out their shoes on St. Nicholas's Eve in hopes of finding them filled with gifts and sweets. In Holland, clogs are left on the hearth for St. Nicholas, with a bit of hay and lumps of sugar for his steed. In Italy, it is an old woman, La Befana, who comes on Epiphany Eve with her bag of treats. In Spain, shoes are left on the balcony, so that the three kings will fill them. But here

BEADED STOCKINGS
A parade of luxurious cashmere stockings (opposite) sparkle with silver-lined bugle beads that have been stitched on. The stockings hang under the mantel from pairs of cashmere "laces" tied in bold knots (see page 19). Choose patterns like pinstripes, blanket stitches, or snowflakes (above) for stockings that will endure from one generation to the next. For complete instructions, see pages 16 through 19.

in America, during the early 1800s, St. Nicholas became Santa Claus, he turned in his white steed for reindeer and a sleigh, and started filling stockings. "Twas the night before Christmas" was written in New York City in 1822, capturing the public imagination almost immediately, and since then we have hung our stockings by the chimney with care. ✷ But the beauty of handmade stockings isn't just for Christmas Eve enjoyment. Make a gift of elegant cashmere stockings, with hand-sewn silver-lined beads in holiday motifs, or crisp handkerchief-linen stockings, to serve as a decorative display throughout the season. And stockings needn't be confined to just mantelpieces: Strung along a footboard or a stair landing, they can fill the house with anticipation. ✷ Stockings stuffed with presents make charming personalized gifts for friends with special interests. An oilcloth stocking can be filled with a fly-fisherman's tackle; a sturdy earth-colored stocking may contain gloves, seeds, and small hand tools for the avid gardener. For almost any hobbyist—cook, bird-watcher, or painter—you can find the appropriate stocking fabric and small trinkets to nestle inside. ✷ Old sweaters are perhaps the loveliest and easiest of foundations for gift stockings. Cut from a template, each sweater's distinctive embellishments, such as the placket, buttons, collars, and neck trims, provide all the adornments a stocking needs. With a few simple stitches, they will be ready to present and to hang on Christmas Eve, the perfect catchall for any overloaded Santa.

SPECIALTY STOCKINGS
Give a gift that is tailor-made to a loved one's fancy—the stocking fabric hints at what's inside. Opposite, clockwise from top left: Shower stockings, made of terry cloth and waffle-weave fabric, can hold soap, body wash, bath bubbles, scent, brushes, a comb, cotton swabs, cotton balls, a loofah, and nail polish. For the fly fisherman, an oilcloth stocking rimmed with flies is filled with a reel, a box of flies, a book on fishing, sinkers, a cork and plastic bobbers, and a compass. A natural-linen stocking, personalized with an herb marker, is packed with presents to delight any gardner: seeds, twine, terra-cotta pots, garden tags, gloves, pruners and sheers, hand salve, bug repellent, and a flower frog. Sew looped ribbons onto striped socks, and fill them with gifts to keep shoes shining bright: a chamois, polish, saddle soap, brushes, a shoehorn, shoe laces, and applicators. See page 16 for how to make these and a cook's stocking.

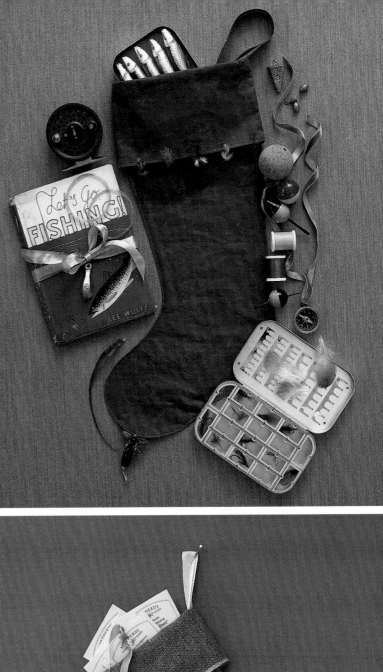

SEWING A BASIC STOCKING

self cuff and attached cuff

For all the stocking directions found on this page and pages 17, 18, and 19, you will need fabric, our basic-stocking template on page 133, a sewing marking pencil or tailor's chalk, sewing shears, straight pins, needle and thread, and a sewing machine.

SELF-CUFF STOCKING Follow these directions to make the cashmere stockings on page 12. Using the stocking template, pin template to wrong side of fabric. With a sewing marking pencil or tailor's chalk, trace template to fabric. Repeat for back side of stocking. Follow instructions on page 18 for embroidering a snowflake on stocking. Cut out. 1. Stitch around the stocking from notch to notch, wrong sides facing, leaving a ¼-inch seam allowance. So seams will lay smoothly around the curved edges of the stocking, cut notches into fabric about $\frac{1}{16}$ inch from seam at the ankle, toe, and heel. 2. Turn stocking right-side out. With wrong sides together, stitch from notch to top of stocking on each side. Press cuff seams open. With right sides together, hand stitch a ½-inch hem around the rim of the cuff. Fold cuff down so that the seam connecting the stocking and cuff is completely covered.

ATTACHED-CUFF STOCKING This cheerful, practical cook's stocking (left) will delight any chef. The stocking, made with an attached cuff, is easy to make from kitchen towels or ticking fabric. It contains wooden spoons, a pepper grinder, tongs, a Japanese kitchen knife, a vegetable peeler, salt spoons, coarse salt, vanilla beans, a grater, and truffle oil. Follow these instructions to make the shower, fisherman, and gardener stockings on page 15 and the handkerchief stockings on page 21. Using the basic-stocking and attached-cuff templates on page 133, fold fabric to double thickness, right sides together. Pin the templates to fabric. With a sewing marking pencil or tailor's chalk, trace the templates onto fabric. Pin the stocking pieces together, right sides facing, and cut out. 1. Leaving a ¼-inch seam allowance, stitch around the stocking, leaving the top open. Remove all the pins. So seams will lay smoothly around the curved edges of the stocking, cut notches into fabric about $\frac{1}{16}$ inch from the seam at the front ankle, toe, and heel. To make the cuff, stitch the short sides of the cuff fabric together, leaving a ¼-inch seam allowance. Press open seams. Slip the cuff over the stocking with all seams facing out. Align cuff seam with seam on heel side of stocking, and stitch the top edges of the cuff and stocking together, leaving a ¼-inch seam allowance. Press seams open. 2. Turn the stocking right-side out. Hand stitch a ½-inch hem around the rim of the cuff. Fold the cuff down so that the seams connecting the stocking and cuff are completely covered. Press if necessary.

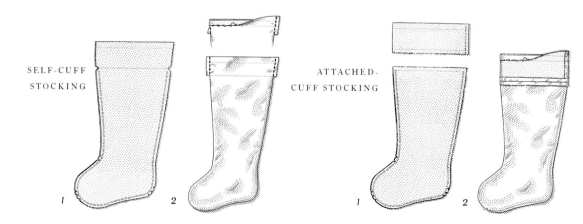

SELF-CUFF
STOCKING

1

2

ATTACHED-
CUFF STOCKING

1

2

MAKING A ONE-OF-A KIND STOCKING

use a sweater or a handkerchief

SWEATER STOCKING Sweaters with unique pockets, collars, or buttons make excellent stockings. Cutting a stocking from a patterned sweater gives the illusion that you knit it yourself. Use the wide-ribbed bottom of a sweater to make the cuff (below right). Place basic-stocking template on page 133 on sweater, positioning it so that buttons are centered, pockets do not fall into seams, and collars are incorporated by laying pattern flush with shoulders of sweater (below left). Pin through front and back of sweater. Cut out stocking shape through both layers (we elongated the toe for stockings on page 20). Be sure to center the part of the sweater you wish to emphasize. Follow stocking instructions for the attached-cuff stocking on page 16. For the pocket stocking (page 20), use the attached-cuff template (page 133), and make a template for the toe, using our basic-stocking template (page 133) as a guide. Pin and trace templates onto wool or felt; cut out. With right sides facing, stitch around curve of toe, leaving a ¼-inch seam allowance. Press seams open, turn right side out, and hand stitch to right side of stocking. With right sides together, stitch short sides of cuff together. Press seams open, turn right side out, and hand stitch to right side of stocking. For the cardigan stockings (page 20), top of stocking should be wide enough to fit neck of sweater with a ¼-inch seam allowance on each side. Adjust stocking template to accommodate sweater's neck.

HANDKERCHIEF STOCKING Look for monogrammed and patterned handkerchiefs at flea markets and tag sales. When deciding the size of your stocking, be sure that its opening is neither too big nor too small to accept the folded handkerchief that will be sewn to the top of the stocking. You will need Swiss-dot cotton or handkerchief linen, a handkerchief, our basic-stocking and cuff templates on page 133, straight pins, a tape measure, needle and thread, sewing shears, and a sewing machine. Follow instructions for making a stocking with an attached cuff (opposite). To make handkerchief cuff, fold handkerchief, right sides facing, and pin cuff template onto fabric. Position template so that decorative part of handkerchief and a finished edge are incorporated. Proceed with instructions for attaching cuff. Because the handkerchief already has a finished edge, there is no need to stitch a hem around the cuff. Turn the stocking right-side out, drape cuff over stocking, and press if necessary.

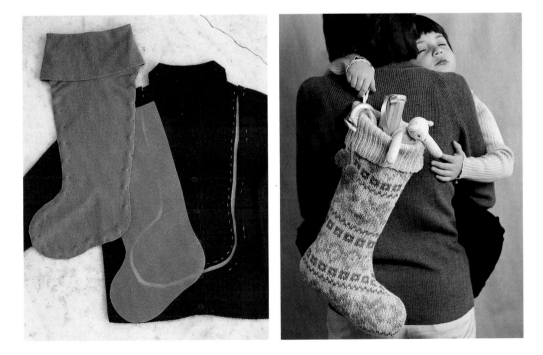

EMBROIDERING STOCKINGS WITH BEADS

snowflakes, laces, pinstripes, and blanket stitches

The beaded stockings on pages 12 and 13 are made with a self cuff. To sew them, follow the instructions for the self-cuff stocking on page 16. See the bead glossary (below left) to help guide you in making the snowflake and pinstripe stockings.

LARGE SNOWFLAKES To make the snowflake stocking on page 12 and at left, you'll need: 35mm and 12mm bugle beads; 10/0 and 5/0 rocaille beads; the large snowflake template on page 132; the basic-stocking template on page 133; a 10-inch embroidery hoop; a sewing marking pencil or tailor's chalk; embroidery scissors; and a needle and thread. 1. Trace stocking template to wrong side of fabric using sewing pencil or tailor's chalk. Place snowflake template in center of stocking on wrong side. Pierce each point with a pin. Using sewing pencil, mark points onto fabric. 2. Position fabric in embroidery hoop with star in center of stocking. Embroider the six long branches of snowflake first. Working from wrong side of fabric, push a threaded needle through to right side of fabric at center of snowflake. Sew a 5/0 rocaille bead onto center point. Working down a branch, sew on a 35mm bugle bead and a 12mm bugle bead; finish the tip of the branch with a 10/0 rocaille bead. Knot thread. For the inner six-pointed star, follow the technique above to sew two 12mm bugle beads at an angle off of adjacent branches one-quarter of the way down each branch. Beads will meet to form a point. Sew a 10/0 rocaille bead at point. Repeat between each branch. Following the template, sew two 12mm bugle beads at an angle on either side of the middle of branch and again at three-quarters of the length of each branch. Finish the tip of each with a 10/0 rocaille bead. Repeat for each of the five remaining branches.

SMALL SNOWFLAKES For the stocking with four snowflakes, also on page 13, follow the process above using the small snowflake template on page 132 and 25mm and 6mm bugle beads and 10/0 and 5/0 rocaille beads.

BEAD GLOSSARY

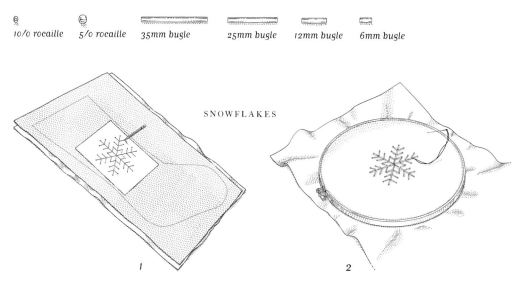

10/0 rocaille   5/0 rocaille   35mm bugle   25mm bugle   12mm bugle   6mm bugle

SNOWFLAKES

1

2

STOCKING LACES To make the loose knot on pages 12 and 13, cut two twelve ½-by-3-inch pieces of fabric. Fold one rectangle lengthwise with right sides facing. Sew long side and one short side together, leaving a ¼-inch seam allowance. Turn right side out, leaving edges of open end raw. Repeat with second rectangle. Tack one "lace" on either side of seam on heel side of stocking at length you wish, and tie.

NARROW PINSTRIPES For the many-striped stocking on page 12, you'll need 35mm bugle beads; 25 mm bugle beads; 12mm bugle beads; 5/0 rocailles; a rectangular picture frame the length of stocking; basic-stocking template (page 133); thumbtacks; a tape measure; a ruler; embroidery scissors; a sewing marking pencil; and needle and thread. Trace stocking template on wrong side of fabric. Using marking pencil and ruler, draw a horizontal line between notches. Mark center of line; draw a vertical line from it down middle of stocking. Measure, mark, and draw remaining pinstripes ¾ inch apart. 1. Position fabric, right side up, on picture frame; secure with thumbtacks. Do not pull fabric. Starting at heel, measure ½ inch from bottom of stocking, push needle through from wrong side, slip on a rocaille, a 35mm bugle bead, a rocaille, a 25mm bugle bead, a rocaille, and a 12mm bugle bead; sew onto right side, following pinstripe down on wrong side. Repeat until beaded pinstripe is ¼ inch from the horizontal line at top. 2. Tack pinstripe down at every third rocaille. Repeat for remaining pinstripes, always starting with a rocaille. Stop beading stripe nearest the tip of the toe ½ inch from tip of toe. Repeat for back side of stocking.

WIDE PINSTRIPES For the wide-striped stocking on page 12, you'll need seven strands of rocaille beads and the items used for making narrow pinstripes (above). Trace stocking template on wrong side of fabric. Draw a horizontal line between two notches. Mark center of line; draw a vertical line to bottom of stocking. Using a tape measure and pencil, measure, mark, and draw remaining pinstripes ½ inch apart. 1. Position fabric, right side up, on picture frame; secure with thumbtacks. Holding a strand of rocaille beads, tie a knot at one end and thread other into needle. Starting at heel on right side of fabric, ½ inch from bottom of stocking, push needle through to wrong side of fabric, leaving one inch of thread. Knot thread on wrong side, leaving ½ inch of thread. 2. Tack rocaille strand along pinstripe at ¾-inch intervals, always starting and finishing on wrong side of fabric. Tack beads to within ¼ inch of horizontal line, remove excess beads, sew thread through to wrong side, and knot.

BLANKET STITCHES To make this shiny seamlike edge (see stocking on page 12, far right), you'll need a needle and thread, 12mm bugle beads, and a finished stocking (see template, page 133). 1. Beginning on inside of stocking, ¼ inch below notch at top of toe side, push out needle through seam, slip on two beads, and insert needle down into fabric, one bead's length from edge. Bring needle out at the edge, keeping thread loop under needle. Continue around stocking, stopping ¼ inch below notch at the top of the heel side of the stocking.

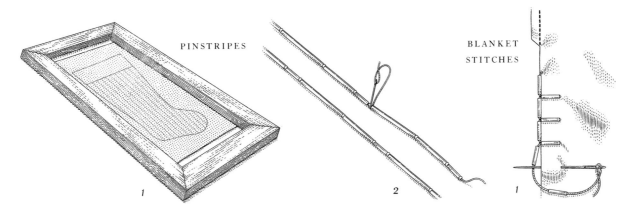

PINSTRIPES

BLANKET STITCHES

1   2   1

HEIRLOOM STOCKINGS
*Revive an old sweater by
making a stocking from its
prettiest parts. Stockings made
from cardigans (below, center
and right) need no embellishment. Their collars are the
stockings' cuffs, their buttons
the decorations. The chest
pocket of a pullover becomes a
handy holder for candy on a
ribbed-sweater stocking (left).
Five winter-white stockings
grace the foot of a Louis XVI-
style daybed (opposite), their
handkerchief cuffs attached
to Swiss-dot cotton and handkerchief-linen fabric. For
instructions for all of these
stockings, see page 17.*

Christmas
cards are for
contemplating
and for
keeping—and
for creating

TURNING
CARDS
INTO
KEEPSAKES

Holiday cards are like snowflakes. They come by ones and twos at first, silently falling into our mailboxes, delightful harbingers of the season. Then comes the winter storm, a blizzard of greetings, and with scant attention to their individual beauty, we pile them into baskets and

drawers and crowd them onto mantels and shelves. ✳ But cards deserve more than a moment. Holiday cards are the first gifts of the season, more precious now, perhaps, than ever. How welcome, amid all the clutter in our mailboxes, to find envelopes from faraway family or friends with a few all-too-rare handwritten lines. ✳ Each card is a unique bearer

of seasonal beauty. Have you noticed that, like snowflakes, no two are exactly alike? Cards are a ready resource for decorating, as festive as any wreath, garland, or string of lights. On these pages are a host of clever ways to arrange your cards, to transform an empty wall space, door, or tabletop into a vibrant display of seasonal motifs, colors, and designs. With a little care and preparation,

HOLIDAY HOUSE OF CARDS *Construct a cozy cottage or modernist skyscraper with interlocking cards made from the fronts of old Christmas cards (opposite). Lay a stack of extra cards nearby for guests to play with. For instructions, see page 27. To package the cards as a gift, tie them together at the slits with slender ribbons. Place the deck in a box lined with colored tissue paper (above) and wrap ribbon around the package.*

you will happily handle the deluge, finding in each day's post new additions to your mini gallery. ✳ A holiday bulletin board is easy to fashion and can be a perennial fixture in your home. Covered in crimson fabric and crisscrossing satin ribbons, it provides a lovely backdrop and secure mounting for dozens of cards. Or gather bare branches from the winter woods, arrange them in a vase, and watch your tabletop greetings tree blossom with cards hung from ribbon. Make a dramatic display for cards on the back of a door by hanging shimmering streamers of wide ribbon with sewn-on clips; they also make marvelous small gifts. A color-coordinated selection of cards can also be displayed as an elegant garland, attached to a sash of sheer ribbon and draped underneath a mantel. ✳ After being displayed, cards in all their beauty can be imaginatively incorporated into a variety of holiday heirlooms. Geodesic globes, assembled from dozens of small circles cut from cards, make eye-catching ornaments. Colorful swatches from old cards can also be used to cover little matchboxes. Filled with tiny

gifts and candies, then assembled into a hand-made Advent calendar, the boxes bring weeks of suspense and delight to the holiday household. And don't forget about last year's cards as you wrap this year's presents. Cutouts of reindeer and Santa, mistletoe and snowmen make light-hearted gift tags and decorations for packages.

MATCHBOX ADVENT CALENDAR *Add an Advent calendar (opposite) to your heirloom decorations. Twenty-four matchboxes, one for each day before Christmas, are filled with gifts that can vary from year to year. The boxes, decorated with images cut from old Christmas cards, are threaded onto ribbons tacked to a bulletin board. Evergreen and satin ribbon embellish the board. Slide open a box and find candy, an eraser, colored pencils, a magnifying glass, or a movie ticket (below). For how-to, see page 27.*

HOLIDAY-CARD ORNAMENTS *These plump paper ornaments are surprisingly easy to make. Each ball is made of twenty circles cut from the fronts and inside greetings of Christmas cards. Hang them on doorknobs, furniture keys, or a Christmas tree. Attach them to presents, or wrap them in colorful tissue and tuck into boxes as gifts. For instructions, see opposite page.*

CREATING KEEPSAKES FROM CARDS

house of cards, matchbox calendar, card ornaments

HOLIDAY HOUSE OF CARDS Turn old cards into something new—again and again, since you can reconfigure these interlocking cards whenever you like. They are inspired by the House of Cards, a classic toy created by the American designers Charles and Ray Eames in the fifties. To make the house, you'll need a utility knife, cardboard, a ruler, scissors, wrapping paper, Spray Mount adhesive, and card stock. Use the utility knife (right) to make a cardboard template in the dimensions shown on page 136; make the slits wider than just a single slice. Cut off the back flaps of the cards, and discard. Trim all the cards to the size of the template. To cover the plain sides of the card fronts, cover them with wrapping paper (this is a good way to use scraps too small for wrapping a gift): Spray the plain side of the card with the Spray Mount adhesive (be sure to work in a well-ventilated area), and apply the wrapping paper. Trim the edges of the wrapping paper. If any of your cards are very thin, back them with card stock instead of wrapping paper. Using the template as a guide, cut slits in the cards. Build a holiday house of cards on a side table or a coffee table, or use it as a centerpiece on your holiday dinner table.

MATCHBOX ADVENT CALENDAR Choose your favorite images from old Christmas cards to cover matchboxes for an Advent calendar. To make, you'll need twenty-four matchboxes, Christmas cards, scissors or a utility knife, a ruler, a bone folder (available at art-supply stores), craft glue, narrow ribbon, a square bulletin board, cloth (we used linen), upholstery tacks, greenery sprigs, and small gifts. Cut out a rectangle from each card, sized to wrap around each matchbox (below left). Use the bone folder to score each rectangle at the four places to be folded and to help smooth creases; sharp creases will help rectangle lie flat. Apply glue to back of each rectangle. Lay, glue-side down, on matchbox; position images so they'll appear as you wish on front. Wrap rectangle around matchbox, lining up scored corners with edges of matchbox. Make two horizontal slits in the middle of the back of each cover; thread lengths of narrow ribbon through the slits, securing each with glue. Write numbers on the front of each cover, one through twenty-four. Cover the bulletin board with cloth. Place a small bow at the top of each ribbon; use a tack to hang them from the board. Decorate perimeter of board with complementary ribbons secured with tacks. Attach greenery and a ribbon at the top of the board. Fill each matchbox with small gifts.

HOLIDAY-CARD ORNAMENTS To make these ornamental balls, you'll need scissors, old holiday cards, a 1¼-inch hole punch, cardboard, a ruler, clear-drying craft glue, and silver thread. Cut out twenty circles for each ball: For a small ball, use the hole punch; for a large one, trace around the bottom of a glass (below right). Cut one more circle from cardboard; draw an equilateral triangle, points touching the circumference. Cut out triangle; trace it onto the inside of each circle. Score and fold along all the lines. Next, use the craft glue to join one flap from

each of two circles; triangles should point in the same direction. Using the same technique, attach three more circles to these two, forming what will be the top. Make the bottom the same way. Glue ten remaining circles together, triangle points alternating up and down, forming a line. Glue two end flaps to form what will be the middle section, then glue top and bottom to its flaps. Hang from silver thread.

GREETINGS TREE *Hung with cards-turned-ornaments, a tree of dried branches in a galvanized bucket is the focal point of a hall table (right). Decorate your tree at the beginning of the season with cards from the previous year. Or keep a supply of ribbons and beads on hand, and watch your tree blossom anew after each day's mail arrives. To give this as a gift, assemble the supplies for creating ornaments from cards together with a finished ornament in a wooden box (left), and include instructions for making the greetings tree.*

HOW TO MAKE THE TREE *Collect dried branches and arrange them in a bucket or vase; no water is needed. Next you'll need a hole punch, cards, ribbon, and beads (left). We hung our cards from ribbons whose colors blend well with the branches. Punch a hole through the top of a closed card. String ribbon through the hole, then thread both ends through a bead or two. Tie the ends in a knot or bow. You can also tie a tassel to the ribbon inside the card to hang down. Or punch two holes side by side at the top of the card, thread ribbon ends through from the back, and tie a small bow in front.*

CARD GARLAND Collect your very best cards, and create an elegant decoration to put up year after year (above). We used a selection of white cards in graduating sizes. You'll need a piece of wide ribbon (this sheer silver ribbon is 7 3/4 inches wide) that is long enough to drape beneath the mantel with trailing ends, a 1-inch-wide ribbon of the same length, and a piece of 1-inch-wide ribbon for each card. Wrap a ribbon around the spine of each card so that it is not too loose and not too taut, and knot at the bottom. String the long, thin ribbon through the ribbons at the top of each card. Hang the wider ribbon and card garland from the mantel, and space the cards evenly. If you use satin ribbon and the cards slide toward the center, use pins to keep them in place.

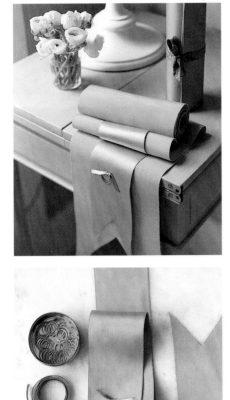

RIBBON STREAMERS *Transform a door into a card gallery (above); to do so, you'll need scissors, lengths of wide ribbon, a ruler, double-ring paper clips, needle and thread, and flat thumbtacks. Cut ribbon to fit your door; we used 4-inch-wide satin ribbons (the middle ribbon is draped atop a 6½-inch-wide ribbon). Mark points on the ribbon where you want to hang cards. Tie thin ribbon to the paper clips (above left). Stitch the clips to the marks you made on the streamers. Fasten ribbon ends to top of door with thumbtacks; slip cards into clips. A roll of ribbon streamers with instructions for displaying cards makes a delightful gift (top left). Cut a thin piece of card stock slightly wider and longer than the streamer. Glue pretty fabric to both sides of card stock. Roll fabric-covered card stock around streamer; secure with ribbon.*

CREATING A HOLIDAY BULLETIN BOARD

A showcase for Christmas cards to put up in early December

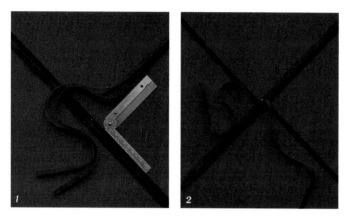

CHRISTMAS BULLETIN BOARD Bring out this special board during the holidays to replace a hall mirror or other prominent piece (opposite), or hang it from a closet door near an entry. For the ribbons and fabric, choose strong colors to show off the cards; if you use one color in different shades, as we did, make sure there is enough contrast between the ribbons and background to differentiate them. We hung our bulletin board above a table set for writing, with various Christmas cards, envelopes, an address book, and pens in a box. When the day's mail arrives, make a list of the people who sent cards, store the list in the box, and slip the newly received cards under the bulletin board's velvet ribbons (below right).

CONSTRUCTING THE BOARD For this project, you'll need a Homasote or compressed-paper board cut to size; sturdy fabric cut 5 inches larger than the board on each side; a staple gun; two lengths of ¼-inch-wide velvet ribbon in two colors; upholstery tacks; a hammer; craft glue or glue gun; a right-angle ruler; and tailor's chalk. If possible, make this project a two-person job: One person pulls the ribbons taut; the other weaves them and secures them with tacks. With a staple gun, attach one fabric edge to the back of the board, then the opposite edge, then the two remaining edges. Using the chalk, outline a pattern for the ribbon on the fabric. Cut two lengths of the ribbon for each drawn line. Then: 1. Lay a pair of ribbons along one chalked line; where lines intersect, hammer an upholstery tack through each ribbon, on opposite sides of the line. Using the right-angle ruler, lay two ribbons along lines that intersect, and weave them into the first pair, hiding the tacks. 2. Tack down two new ribbons where first ribbons overlap them. 3. At each intersection, there are four nails—all concealed by a layer of ribbon. Continue weaving and tacking ribbons. Tack and trim them where they meet the outlined border. 4. Use craft glue or a glue gun to attach more ribbons to the border, stapling the ends on the back of the board. 5. Make sure the ribbons are taut, since they will hold the cards in place. To make a board with ribbons attached as on the border of the Matchbox Advent Calendar (page 25), use ½-inch-wide velvet ribbon and decorative upholstery tacks. Cut just one length of ribbon for each chalk line.

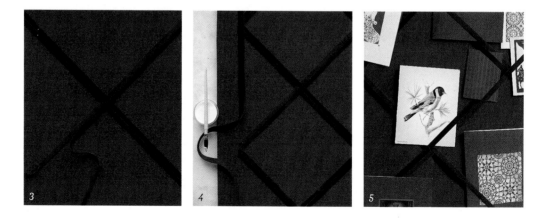

Cherished symbols of cheer herald the holiday year after year

ORNAMENTS AND EVERLASTING WREATHS

As you squeeze the tree through the doorway and the piney smell from a few crushed needles begins to perfume the house, you are probably not thinking of winter rituals that are thousands of years old. In the midwinter festivals of Rome and other ancient cultures, evergreen branches and

garlands were brought inside, to serve as symbols of enduring life and to ensure a fruitful year. And as you illuminate the tree with bright bulbs and reflective baubles, you're following another custom of great antiquity—bringing light to the darkest time of the year, heralding the return of the sun after the winter solstice. ✳ Perhaps it is also true, as some schol-

ars say, that our centuries-old tradition of trimming the tree with colorful ornaments stems from a powerful legend surrounding the Nativity, one which took root at the end of the first millennium. When Christ was born, the story was told throughout medieval Christendom, all the trees in the forest burst into bloom and bore fruit, despite the snow and ice. For centuries to follow, in many

NESTING BIRD *A hand-made bird trimmed with glass beads, ribbons, and a feather tail tends an aerie holding antique glass "eggs" (opposite). Nimble wire legs clutch the rim of the floral-shop nest, set onto the tree where the branches converge. After the holidays, the bird can be stored in an everlasting "nest" (above). The plain bentwood box is painted pink, lined with slightly crumpled tissue strips, and tied with a wide grosgrain ribbon.*

places around Europe, boughs of dormant cherry and hawthorn—sometimes whole trees or bushes—were brought into flower at Christmas, and forced in water inside the home, as celebration of that miracle. Having the prettiest springlike display of blooms was a source of great pride and friendly competition among neighbors. ✳ So today, as our Christmas trees bloom with lights and garlands, toys, candies, angels, and stars, they connect us with remote forebears, with times and places vastly different from our own. But much closer to home, the festive season of tree trimming is a time to create new traditions, to strengthen the bonds within our own circle of family, friends, and neighbors. ✳ The tree adornments and wreaths that follow can be made with saved and found objects. Short lengths of ribbon from Christmases past can be looped and linked into a colorful ribbon garland, a perfect project to do with children. Scraps of fabric take wing in our beaded birds—make them in different colors, and present them each year to dear friends to increase their flock. Look for jingle bells in various colors and sizes to make a wreath that sounds merrily with every opening of the door. And from the cut-glass facets of old chandeliers, you can create a crystal constellation of stars that will twinkle over the tree each year. ✳ To preserve your decorations or give them as gifts, choose wrappings that will protect them during the months when they are put away. Like the ribbon-lined box for the chandelier stars on page 46, a pretty storage container becomes part of the keepsake, a simple step turning this year's handiwork into cherished heirlooms.

SCARLET WREATH *A fresh cranberry wreath will survive just one Christmas, but this beaded version (opposite), inspired by the fruit ornaments collected by the Victorians, will never lose its vibrancy. The ruby-red glass beads, secured with pins brushed with red nail polish and luxurious red satin ribbon, add a bold stroke of color to a spare setting. The long free ends of the bow and a compote filled with cranberries and plums are the only decoration needed on the mantel. For how-to, see page 45.*

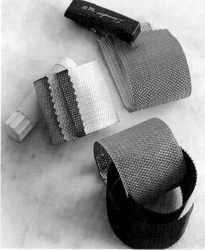

RIBBON TREE *Scraps of ribbon from last year's gifts are artfully recycled into chain-link garlands and ornamental birds on this tabletop tree (above). Lengths of ribbons also frame the hexagonal velvet tree skirt (see page 40). Not only are the ribbon chains easier to preserve than the paper versions that inspired them, but new links can be added year after year. To make the chain, choose ribbons in a variety of widths and textures (top right); splurge on new ribbons if a specific color scheme appeals to you. Cut ribbons into uniform lengths. Staple a length of ribbon together, wrong-side out, just above ends. Glue ends back against the fabric with a glue stick, then turn right-side out. Run another piece of ribbon through this link (bottom right), and repeat the stapling, gluing, and linking process until you've run out of ribbon.*

STITCHING A FABRIC BIRD

a handmade nesting bird will become a family heirloom

FABRIC BIRD To make the bird ornaments seen on pages 34 and 35, you will need fancy fabrics in contrasting colors and textures (we used brocade, velvet, and wide ribbon), polyester stuffing, tiny colored glass beads, a beading needle, a curved upholstery needle, feathers, white craft glue, tiny black glass beads, and 20-gauge floral wire. 1. Using the templates found on page 135, enlarge them to desired size on a photocopier and trace them onto the fabrics. Cut out two body pieces, four wing pieces, and one breast piece. 2. Sew the two sides of the body together leaving a ¼-inch seam allowance, right sides facing, beginning at the tail, over the back, and ending on the throat, at the point indicated by the line on the template, leaving the bottom open. Sew the breast fabric inside out to the body beginning at this line: First lift up one side of body, and stitch the breast in place along entire lower half of the body; then, on the other side, sew from the line for about an inch, and leave a gap of one inch or so before joining the rest of the body to breast fabric. (Do not completely join the two lines of stitching at tail; leave a small hole to insert the feathers.) Use the gap to turn fabric right-side out: Place the head between your thumb and forefinger, and gently separate the two pieces of fabric; poke your finger through the gap and inside the head, and begin to turn fabric right-side out. Push the head toward the gap with a thin, rounded object like a chopstick, until head emerges from

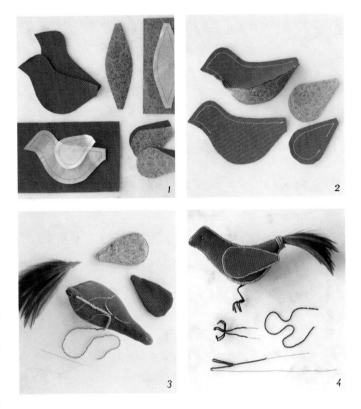

gap. Beginning at the head, fill the bird with the polyester stuffing. Repeat sewing process for wings, which are also sewn together with right sides facing. A similar gap is left on wings (as shown) to turn them right-side out, but they are not filled. Don't attach wings to body until step four. 3. Transfer the strung beads to the beading needle threaded with string in a color that matches the fabric. Use the curved upholstery needle to sew alongside the beads, crossing over every third bead with thread: Begin sewing the beads to the body at the tail, running over the beak and to the breast, where beads will branch to one side of the breast fabric, and end at the tail. Sew restrung beads along unbeaded side of the breast by the same method, and also along the edges of the wings. Knot the string at the end of the restrung beads to prevent them from slipping off. Bunch together the tips of feathers, and glue them to a small triangle of fabric. Dab some glue in the tail-feather hole, and insert feathers. Sew more restrung beads around the tail. 4. Thread the bead eyes through the head several times, knotting off the end of thread. Sew the wings to the body; using the curved upholstery needle, sew downward from the top underside of the wing to the bottom middle of wing. Do not sew the bottom half of the wing to the body. To make the claw, transfer the black beads to the floral wire; when you have transferred several inches of beads, begin looping the wire to form three claws (each formed again into smaller loops at top of claw to keep beads from slipping), as shown in progress, at bottom. Leave the wire open at the ends of the two legs to poke into the bird, and position the leg. Repeat process for a second leg.

MAKING A VELVET TREE SKIRT

use velvet and ribbons to make the bottom of the tree as pretty as the top

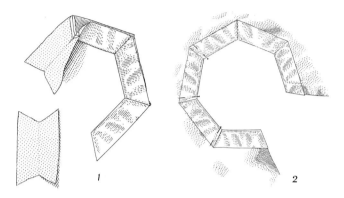

1

2

MAKING THE TREE SKIRT This project requires advanced sewing skills. You will need velvet; 2-inch-wide grosgrain ribbon and thread to match; ¾-inch-wide satin ribbon and thread to match; sewing shears; a needle; a ruler; a protractor; ribbon-binding pattern (left); a sewing marking pencil or tailor's chalk; a square piece of kraft paper at least 26 inches wide; paper scissors; straight pins; an iron and board; a sewing machine; and hooks and eyes. Make a pattern for the hexagonal tree skirt on the kraft paper. Draw a 12-inch line parallel to one side of the paper, about ½ inch from the edge. Use the protractor to make a 125-degree angle off the original line, and draw a 12-inch line from that angle. Repeat for five remaining sides of hexagon. The last line drawn will not meet with the first. With the protractor, make a 62½-degree angle off the first and last lines, and draw a line to the center of the hexagon from each point, forming a small triangle. This will become the opening for the skirt. Cut out the skirt and the triangle. To make the hole for the tree, fold the pattern like an accordion, stacking the lines around the perimeter of the skirt on top of each other to form a triangle. Measure 2 inches from the top of the triangle, draw a straight line across, and cut. Open the pattern. Place the pattern on the wrong side of the velvet. With the marking pencil or tailor's chalk, trace the skirt pattern on the fabric, and cut out. 1. To make the ribbon binding that will line the tree hole, cut out six pieces of grosgrain ribbon by enlarging the template on this page to fit your skirt pattern. Sew them right sides together, one at a time, so the Vs meet. Fold sewn ribbon in half lengthwise, wrong sides together, and press with a hot iron to create a hexagon. 2. Bind the edge of the tree hole with the ribbon. The fabric should fit neatly inside the folded ribbon. Pin in place, and stitch. 3. Fold the rest of the grosgrain ribbon in half, lengthwise, and press. Starting from the opening, wrap the ribbon around the outer edge of skirt, and pin. For a sharp corner, smooth the fabric so it lies flat, and press. Continue around the perimeter of skirt, and stitch. 4. Using tailor's chalk, draw a line 1¾ inches from the edge of skirt parallel to each side of hexagon. Cut four 36-inch pieces of satin ribbon and two 24-inch pieces for the first and last sides of skirt. Beginning at the opening of the skirt, pin a short piece of satin ribbon along the drawn line. For the first and last pieces, do not cut the excess ribbon; for other pieces, position them so that they are equal lengths of excess ribbon on both sides. Stitch top and bottom edges of ribbon, stopping about ¼ inch from each bend in the skirt so that the ribbons can be tied into knots or bows. Trim all edges evenly. 5. Pin the remaining grosgrain ribbon to the unfinished edges at the opening of the skirt, tucking raw edges of ribbons under themselves. 6. Stitch, and secure opening with hooks and eyes.

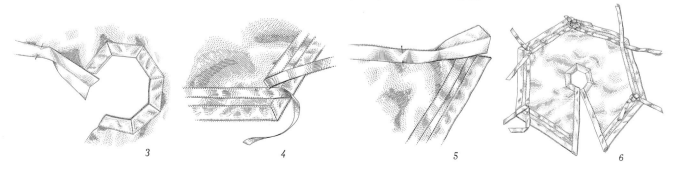

3

4

5

6

TINSEL TREE TOPPER *This traditional Christmas star (above) and the eight-pointed one on page 11 become shimmering beacons when coated with silver glitter and outlined with wired tinsel roping or silver metallic cord. See page 44 for instructions. To store or give as a gift, swaddle a star in delicate tissue and tuck into a box sturdy enough to last for generations of Christmases.*

SILVERY KEEPSAKES
The sound of sleigh bells need not be reserved for one night a year. Hang this wreath of jingle bells on a door handle and enjoy the familiar ring throughout the season. To make it, see page 45. Crafted from origami paper, these shimmering silver ornaments (opposite) make a Christmas tree magical, but are just as radiant dangling from a window. For instructions, see page 44.

CRAFTING DECORATIONS THAT SPARKLE AND SHINE

origami ornaments and glittery stars

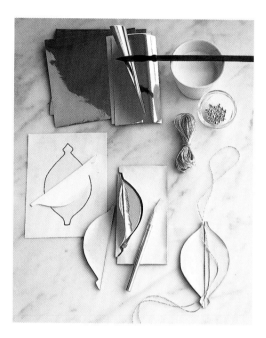

ORIGAMI ORNAMENTS For the ornaments on page 42, you'll need fifty sheets of 6-inch-square silver origami paper; craft glue; a utility knife; a 40-inch length of silver embroidery floss; a needle threader; templates on page 134 (enlarge on a photocopier to no bigger than 7 inches); and beads. Fold each sheet of paper in half, shiny sides in. Keeping sheets folded, divide into two groups of twenty-five. Brush glue over the nonshiny half of one sheet. Place nonshiny half of another sheet on top of glued one; the folded edges of the sheets should be aligned. Smooth. Repeat until two 25-sheet stacks have been formed. Let dry. Choose a template. Cut out shape, then cut on dotted line; you'll only need half. Lay template on each stack; cut out shape with utility knife. Glue the backs of bottom sheets of each stack together, forming one stack. In the middle of the newly combined stack, open one folded sheet. Turn stack over, laying the open sheet flat and facedown. There will be a groove down the middle of the side that's facing up. Fold floss in half, and lay along groove. Glue in place, with the loop of floss extending above the ornament for a hanger. Glue backs of top and bottom sheets of the combined stack together covering floss and creating a fan effect. Using a needle threader, attach beads to top and bottom of floss; tie off. Open the ornament leaf by leaf.

GLITTERY STAR For the stars on page 11 and 41, you'll need 14-gauge galvanized utility wire; a dowel; wire cutters; two pieces of paper (in a dark, neutral color, corrugated on one side) per star; a utility knife; heavy tissue; spray adhesive; coarse glitter; a hot-glue gun; and wired tinsel for five-pointed star (silver metallic cord for eight-pointed star). Beginning 8 inches from the end of a piece of utility wire, make a coil 3½ to 4 inches long around dowel; dowel's diameter should equal that of the vertical branch at top of tree. Snip wire at end of coils. Remove from dowel. **1.** Using templates on page 132, cut two of the same star shapes out of corrugated paper. On smooth side of one piece, locate center by connecting opposite points of star with five ruler-guided pencil-drawn lines; make a pinhole where lines intersect. Beginning at pinhole and using the ruler, score lines by lightly cutting to just beneath the smooth surface of paper along the long lines with utility knife. Turn star over. Repeat scoring along the short lines to just beneath corrugated surface. With smooth side facing up again, push down on short scored lines and up (from beneath)

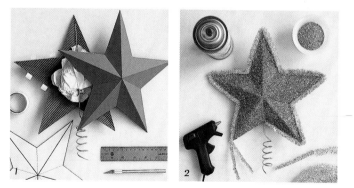

on long scored lines. Paper will be three-dimensional. Repeat on other star shape. Crumple tissue; place in center of one star half. Run straight end of coiled wire through crumpled tissue. Place tape along all points of star; tape halves together. **2.** Coat both sides of star with adhesive; sprinkle with glitter. Attach tinsel or cord to sides of star with hot-glue gun.

MAKING EVERLASTING WREATHS

jingle-bell wreath and beaded-cranberry wreath

JINGLE-BELL WREATH The jingle bell wreath on page 42 is easy to make and will last forever. To make it, you will need a length of 16-gauge wire (ours is approximately 30 inches), needle-nose pliers, jingle bells in different colors and sizes (we used approximately 75), a length of wide satin ribbon, and 24-gauge wire. Shape the 16-gauge wire into a circle for the wreath form. Make a closed loop at one end of the wire with the needle-nose pliers. Thread the jingle bells in desired order onto the open wire end (right). When the wire is full with bells, join its ends by twisting the unlooped end into a hook, and fasten it onto the closed loop. Tie the satin ribbon into a bow, and secure it to the bottom of the wreath with the 24-gauge wire. Hang the finished wreath on any inside door that is frequently used, such as a front door, a coat-closet door, or even a kitchen cupboard.

BEADED CRANBERRY WREATH The vivid beaded wreath on page 37 looks as handsome hanging from a window or wall as it does from a mirror. To make it, you will need a 10" tubular Styrofoam wreath form; red nail polish; red seam binding; red druk beads in 6mm, 8mm, and 10mm sizes (we used approximately 360); flat-head straight pins (one for each bead); and white craft glue. Paint the heads of the pins with the red nail polish so the silver tips will not show on the wreath; to complete this step quickly, stick the pins into a strip of paper or Styrofoam, and brush the polish along the pin tops. Let dry completely. 1. Wrap the Styrofoam wreath form with the red seam binding, securing with straight pins at the beginning and end. Be sure the seam binding overlaps slightly to cover the Styrofoam completely. 2. To cover the wreath with beads, slip a bead onto a polish-painted pin, dab the sharp tip of the pin in a dish of craft glue, and push the pin into the wrapped Styrofoam form. Pin the larger beads onto the wreath first, then fill in any gaps with the smaller beads. 3. Cluster the beads so they do not appear to be too evenly spaced. Continue until the front and the sides of the wreath are covered with beads. Leave the back of the wreath plain. To make the bow for a wreath to be placed over a mantel, loop an extra-long piece of the satin ribbon around the bottom of the wreath, and tie it into a loose bow, leaving the ends long so they drape naturally. To finish, cut the ends in a V. To hang it, attach a piece of double-sided wide satin ribbon in a coordinating color to the back of the wreath with the flat-head pins.

DESIGNING ORNAMENTS FROM CHANDELIER PIECES

sparkling decorations to suspend from the ceiling and hang on the tree

CRYSTAL STARS A constellation of stars hung from the ceiling by fishing line tops a tree trimmed with Christmas balls, beaded garlands, and icicles (opposite). In the middle of the constellation is the largest star, made by gluing together old chandelier pieces found at a flea market. Surrounding it are single chandelier pieces and smaller three-dimensional stars. Centered on a 1940s Venetian-style mirrored table, the tree is swathed in a piece of iridescent velvet fabric gracefully wrapped around the base. The gifts, tied with metallic silver ribbon, are wrapped to echo the colors and textures of the tree. A pair of Louis XVI chairs and antique Murano sconces frame the glistening tree. Chandelier ornaments are easy and fun to put together, and no two are exactly alike. Why not give a friend the opportunity to create these spectacular decorations? To create a gift box for these jewels (left), glue a piece of ribbon around the perimeter of an unpainted balsa wood box (available at crafts stores), and line the inside with wide silk-satin moiré ribbon. Fill the box with chandelier pieces (wipe them with heavy-duty glass cleaner first), and include instructions.

MAKING CHANDELIER-PIECE ORNAMENTS To make these ornaments, you can use chandelier pieces of any size. Small pieces can be glued together to form stars like the tall sparkler suspended over the tree. You'll also need needle-nose pliers; a heavy-duty glass cleaner; a thin skewer; clear-drying glass adhesive; fishing line; and an eye hook. Before gluing pieces together, remove wires and loops with pliers. Soak pieces overnight in glass cleaner. 1. To make an ornament from small pieces, lay out pieces and decide on shape you want the ornament to be. For the snowflake, we used a large octagonal piece to create the center. Pieces will first be attached to center, then extended piece by piece. Using skewer, apply adhesive to edge of one piece; press onto center piece. Let dry. Continue attaching pieces. Wrap fishing line around center piece, tie off in back, and hang over center of tree from an eye hook in the ceiling. Smaller chandelier ornaments can be hung from thumbtacks. 2. Larger chandelier pieces make lovely ornaments on their own. To hang them, thread a single piece of 28-gauge wire through hole in the middle of chandelier piece; join ends at top. Using small needle-nose pliers, form a loop with the double strand of wire (top). Still using pliers, wrap double strand around wire below loop (bottom), and cut off excess wire (right). Place an ornament hook through the loop and hang from the tree or ceiling, surrounding a larger ornament. The configuration of stars hanging over the tree is designed to refract light. Place lots of lights at the top of the tree to reflect the sparkling ornaments.

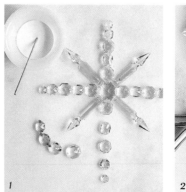

1

2

GIFTS FOR ONE OR MORE

BOWLS TO FILL
WITH STEAMING
HOT CHOCOLATE;
SOFT SLIPPERS
TO SNUGGLE
SMALL TOES—
OUR FAVORITE
GIFTS PROVIDE
WARMTH AND
COMFORT
AGAINST THE
CHILL OF THE
SEASON. SIMPLY
ASSEMBLED OR
SKILLFULLY
STITCHED, THEY
GLOW WITH
THE TOUCH OF
YOUR OWN
HANDS—AND IN
THE ACT OF
CREATION AND
THE RITUAL
OF GIVING, YOU
ARE WARMED
AS WELL.

For some,
only a
unique gift
made
by hand
will do

SPECIAL
GIFTS
FOR ONE

Long before there was Christmas, there were presents. Gift giving is an instinct—a ritual that emerges from the human heart—and it has long been associated with the festivals of the winter solstice. In ancient Rome, during the Saturnalia, rich folk gave generously to the unfortunate and received garlands in return. And the arrival of the new year was marked with exchanges of honeyed treats, lamps, and money, meant to ensure a year of sweetness, light, warmth, and wealth. ✳ Through the millennia, these early customs have become entwined and enriched with religious traditions. And along with all aspects of our culture, gift giving has grown ever more complex. Even a hundred and fifty years ago, Harriet Beecher Stowe captured, in one of her early stories, *Christmas; or the Good Fairy*, a sentiment that many of us feel today: "Oh dear," says a character in the tale, "Christmas is coming in a fortnight, and I have got to think up presents for everybody!" ✳ Today, with the click of a button, you can toss a present into a "virtual" shopping cart. Yes, the Internet is a marvel of convenience and a great boon to busy folks with far-flung families. But sometimes a present that you have not seen, touched, wrapped, and sent yourself just does not feel right. And often, a present that you have bought, though it may be grand and glorious, does not carry with it the personal touch you want to convey. ✳ The answer, some-

DECOUPAGE BOXES
With their lids painted and papered with decorative prints, these wood boxes (opposite) recall the traditional craft of decoupage. The boxes are sanded and finished with pearlized silver paint, which allows the pretty grain of the wood to show through. Tuck a gift inside, or give the lustrous box as a gift itself, tied with narrow or wide ruby-colored ribbon. For complete instructions, see page 54.

times, is to give gifts made the old-fashioned way—with your own hands. The projects in this chapter will show you how easy and rewarding this can be: The gifts can be constructed at your leisure and will truly bring you back in touch with the essential pleasure of creating and giving, and will give you the satisfaction of fashioning fabric, metal, wood, and paper into lasting expressions of friendship and treasured keepsakes. ✳ One art to rediscover for the holidays is monogramming. With a stitched letter, an ordinary object—a plain napkin, a pillowcase, a pair of slippers—becomes custom-made, personal, a keepsake. With letters taken from books of typography, modified with your own design ideas, you can create a monogram style that reflects the recipient of the gift. ✳ Another venerable craft to consider is decoupage, the classic technique of decorating and refinishing surfaces with thematic cutouts. For our luminescent boxes, we found natural motifs in old botanical volumes, photocopied them onto silver paper, and applied them to balsa-wood boxes coated with pearlized paint. Gilding is also a simple but dazzling technique for gifts. Here yellow- and white-gold leaf are used to create shimmering bowls. ✳ The multitalented gift maker will find several projects in the following pages, such as an exquisite diminutive pincushion, sewn from plush velvet, that is set into a mitered base. Or make a delightful display of pressed flowers or leaves in a cheerful breakfast tray that is fashioned from antique or handmade picture frames. However simple or complex, a handmade gift is always a unique expression of your thoughtfulness and taste.

MAGNETIC BULLETIN BOARD *The refrigerator is every household's favorite bulletin board, but it isn't always located in the most convenient place. With the help of a handful of magnet-backed pebbles, a piece of galvanized steel painted with high-gloss latex enamel can become a stylish message board that can be hung anywhere. In addition to smooth rocks, the magnets can be glued to seashells, buttons, or polished coins from other countries. For complete how-to,* *see page 55.*

SILVERING, PAINTING, AND SEWING SPECIAL GIFTS

decoupaged boxes, gilded bowls, a bulletin board, and a velvet pincushion

SILVER GIFTS Lustrous holiday gifts and decorations can be made not just from sterling but from considerably less precious metallic coverings—white and yellow gold leaf and opalescent paint. The art of silvering, originally developed to imitate the real thing, has been practiced by artisans for thousands of years. But as with decoupage, which was originally developed to mimic porcelain and lacquerware, the art of silvering is now valued for itself. Silver leaf is a precious metal that has been pounded to slightly more than four millionths of an inch thick; gold leaf is slightly thinner. Anything this thin is practically paint, and that is the way leaves of silver and gold are used to coat humble materials. The techniques that follow require minimal skill but some patience, and the materials are relatively easy to find.

DECOUPAGED WOODEN BOXES A timeless botanical print or animal image is the perfect embellishment for the wooden boxes on page 50. To make them, you'll need an unfinished wooden box, pearlized paint, silver paper, a utility knife, and white craft glue. First, paint the box with two thin coats of paint. To create a decoupage effect on the lid, photocopy images from books or prints onto silver paper (you can reduce or enlarge a picture to the size you desire). Cut out the image with the utility knife, and when the paint is dry, glue the picture to the top of the box (opposite page, photo 1). To give the box a more finished look, cut a ribbon of silver paper to cover the edge of the lid. Make a hole for the wood-joining stud that's on the lid by pressing the paper against the stud with an eraser to make an impression you can cut out. Glue the paper ribbon around the lid edge, being sure to align the hole in the ribbon with the stud.

GILDED BOWLS These bowls (above left) are finished with 18-karat yellow-gold leaf and 24-karat white-gold leaf, which create a softer effect than silver leaf. Gilded bowls are meant for decoration, to hold pinecones, seashells, or mail—never food. To make them, you'll need water-soluble Japan Gold Size, a clean wooden or ceramic bowl, paper-backed gold leaf, and a dry gilding brush. Wear a dust mask while working—metal leaf shouldn't be inhaled. Brush a thin coat of Japan Gold Size on bowl. Let set 15 minutes, until tacky. Carefully take a sheet of gold leaf, place it metal-side down in the center of the bowl, then rub the paper gently with your fingers until metal has been transferred to bowl; discard backing. Repeat laying and rubbing sheets, overlapping them and working from the center out until the bowl is completely covered (opposite, photo 2). Little bits of metal leaf will be left on the paper backing; use these to fill in holes or cracks. When the surface of the bowl is completely covered, brush with the gilding brush (opposite, photo 3); this step will press down the leaf and break off any loose flakes, giving the bowl a finished look.

MAGNETIC BULLETIN BOARD This handsome bulletin board (page 53) can be painted in whatever color suits the recipient. Purchase a piece of galvanized steel at a roofing-supply store (below, photo 4). Have the store fold back the sharp edges and drill two holes near the top. Smooth the treated steel with fine steel wool to remove any imperfections. Remove oil and dirt from the steel by rubbing it with white vinegar (a sensible alternative to the toxic xylene that many paint-can instructions call for), and let it dry completely. In a well-ventilated area, spray the metal with a water-based primer until it is evenly coated. Once the primer has dried, spray the board with two coats of latex enamel. To complete the board, you'll need several small rocks, a disk-shaped magnet for each, a hot-glue gun, venetian-blind cord, white paint, and a picture nail. Paint the sides of the magnets white, then glue them to the backs of the rocks. Thread the ends of the venetian-blind cord from front to back through the two predrilled holes; tie a knot at each end so the cord can't slip out. Hang the bulletin board from the picture nail. Enclose the picture nail and the magnets with the bulletin board if you're giving this as a gift.

VELVET PINCUSHION This cushion is the ideal place to store your pins and needles (opposite, right). The lightweight wooden base steadies the pincushion, which is filled with emery grain, so your pins and needles will get a sharpening each time you put them away. Make a rectangular paper pattern (ours is 4 3/16 inches wide and 5 3/16 inches long); cut out the rectangle, then round the corners and sides, as shown (below, photo #5). Pin the pattern to two pieces of velvet, right sides facing, and cut out. Sew the two pieces together with a ¼-inch seam allowance, leaving a 1¾-inch gap on one long side. Turn the sewn velvet right-side out, and fill pouch to about ¾ full with emery grain (below, photo 6). Hand-stitch the gap. For the base, we cut a piece of 3/32-inch-thick bass wood to 4 5/8 inches long by 3 ½ inches wide (basswood, available at art-supply stores, can be cut with a utility knife). Using a small miter box to guide the saw (below, photo 7), angle the corners of 3/8-inch quarter-round molding that's been cut to fit the basswood base. Glue the molding to the base, and let dry several hours. Sand the wood, paint with enamel paint, and let dry overnight. Place the sewn pincushion in the base, and tuck in corners until cushion is snug.

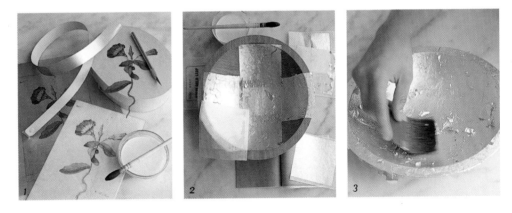

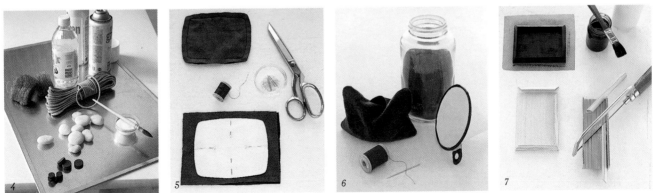

SEWING SWEATER PILLOWS

pillows that look like you knitted them yourself

SWEATER PILLOWS These pillows renew the life of sweaters you've grown tired of wearing (opposite and left). To make one, you'll need a pillow form (available at fabric stores) and a sweater that is a bit larger than the form. Cut two pieces from the sweater, each ½ inch bigger on each side than the pillow form. Choose a section of the sweater with an interesting design or the button-down portion of a cardigan. Handle the cut sweater as little as possible to minimize unraveling. Looser knits will unravel more readily; after cutting, finish sweater edges with a loose zigzag stitch. Pin the pieces together, right sides facing. Using a straight stitch, sew them together on three sides, allowing a ½-inch seam; sew the fourth side only partway, leaving about a 6-inch opening. Turn right-side out, and insert the pillow form. Slip-stitch closed. If making a pillow from a cardigan, stitch all four sides of sweater pieces closed, turn right-side out, open buttons, and insert pillow form (below left). To make a pillow with a welting trim, measure the perimeter of the pillow. Cut the sweater into 2-inch-wide strips. Sew enough strips together, end to end and right sides facing, to trim the pillow. 1. Fold the one long strip lengthwise in half, wrong sides facing, around a length of cording. Using the zipper foot on your sewing machine, stitch along the length of the strip as close to the cording as possible to ensure a snug fit. Trim the raw edges to ½ inch from seam. 2. Pin the welting to the right side of one of the sweater pieces, with welting facing center and raw edges of sweater and the welting flush. Clip notches into the seams where welting rounds the corners so it lies flat. Overlap ends. Stitch in place, following seam line on welting. Lay second sweater piece over this piece, right sides facing; pin. Stitch around the three sides, allowing a ½-inch seam on each side. Sew the fourth side partway, leaving about a 6-inch gap. Trim the corners, turn right-side out, insert pillow form, and slip-stitch closed.

CARDIGAN PILLOW

WELTING

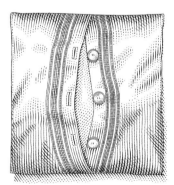

1

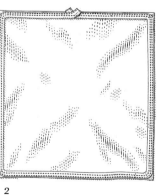

2

GIFTS TO MONOGRAM
Individualize a pair of plain slippers with monogrammed initials; embroider them on covered buttons (top), felt patches tacked to slippers with French knots (middle), or directly on the slippers themselves (bottom). See page 61 for instructions. An assortment of napkins (opposite) shows the possibilities for monogram styles. All were professionally machine embroidered; some are stock fonts, while others were found in old books of type.

HIS-AND-HER PILLOWCASES
Presidential braid is shaped to form letters outlined on a linen pillow sleeve (above); these are the initials of the first names of a couple. Any appropriate initial will look just as lovely. Be sure to choose letters in script style when using presidential braid; it does not form the neat, sharp corners of block-shaped letters. For full instructions, see opposite page.

SILVER-PAPER-MOSAIC FRAME *An inexpensive picture frame becomes as unique as the image inside when squares of silver metallic paper are artfully pieced together to form a mosaic, with the handsome monogram glued onto squares opposite each other (above). Choose a favorite picture, then make this keepsake frame for each set of grandparents, or for a favorite relative, using their initials. The crisp letters of our monogram were chosen to complement the picture frame's strong, clean lines. But there are countless ways to imbue the same set of twenty-six letters with very different personalities. A single character can be lighthearted, authoritative, elegant, or witty; half the fun is choosing the right style for the person to receive the gift. See opposite page for complete instructions.*

MAKING GIFTS WITH MONOGRAMS

slippers, pillowcases, and a frame

GETTING STARTED Even if you do not embroider or sew, you can still make the monogramming projects shown here. Design the monogram yourself, and have a seamstress or professional embroidery shop take care of the rest. Look for letters you love in books of typography (available at libraries and bookstores). Photocopy the letters to the size you want to use as a template (left).

MONOGRAMMED SLIPPERS Initials personalize boiled-wool slippers like the ones on page 59. To make the buttons, draw a circle on felt or melton wool (following instructions on the button kit). Draw a letter in the circle using transfer paper or working freehand. Clip the felt into an embroidery hoop (below left). Use embroidery floss to embroider the letters in satin stitch. Cut out the circle, stretch it over the button, and catch the edges on the teeth in back. Snap the front of the button to the back half, and sew onto a slipper. Use the same method on felt tags, sewing the letters in satin stitch, and securing the patches with French knots. To embroider directly on slippers, transfer lettering or draw freehand onto boiled wool, and use French knots, as we did here, or another favorite stitch.

HIS-AND-HER PILLOWCASES These pillowcases come with contrasting sleeves, but you can also make your own. The initials are outlined in decorative cord called presidential braid. Pin the pattern to the fabric, outline it with a tailor's chalk, then lay the braid in place, and cut it to the precise length (below right). Finish the ends with a dab of glue to keep them from unraveling. Pin braid down, then slip-stitch it in place along both sides.

SILVER-PAPER-MOSAIC FRAME Although a plain picture frame in any size can be used for this project, a flat frame with wide panels works best. Paint front and sides of frame with silver pearlescent paint. Let dry. Decide what size you wish squares to be and where you want to place initials; each side with an initial needs an odd number of squares so initials will be centered. We placed them in the middle of the right and left sides (opposite, left); an alternative is a single initial centered at the top of frame. 1. Cut out squares of metallic silver paper. With a brush, glue silver squares to painted frame with craft glue; do not overlap. Let dry. 2. Choose a typeface you like, and adjust initials to the size you want (we selected a typeface available on a computer). Using a utility knife and a ruler, draw a box around initial; cut out. With a piece of low-tack adhesive tape, attach square to a piece of metallic silver paper that's slightly darker than the silver paper on frame. With a utility knife, carefully cut out initial from dark silver paper. Brush back of it with glue, and glue to a square on frame. Let dry. To protect frame, spray it with clear varnish. Hang from a wide ribbon.

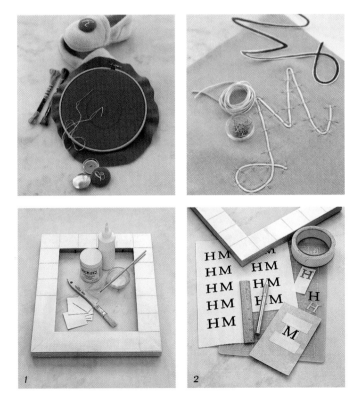

CREATING A PICTURE-FRAME TRAY

a charming showcase for pressed flowers or leaves

PICTURE-FRAME TRAY With a few alterations, a pretty picture frame can become the perfect serving tray. For a plain or unfinished frame, like the box frames found at crafts stores (below), you'll need a piece of ⅛-inch-thick Masonite (available at lumber stores) cut to same size as picture-frame glass, two drawer handles and screws, 1 yard of linen, scissors, artist's tape, pressed flowers (press, facedown, in the middle of a telephone book for 7 to 10 days), ¼-inch quarter-round molding, miter box, razor saw, paint, paintbrush, wood putty, sandpaper, and wood glue. The back of this frame will become the front of the tray (back has deeper lip), so fill in gaps or cover staples with putty; sand to smooth. 1. Cut four lengths of molding: two to inner width of frame, two to inner length. Miter ends at 45-degree angles, making sure angles fit together cleanly. Paint the frame and molding. Attach handles on outside of frame's short sides. 2. Cut a piece of linen 4 inches longer and wider than Masonite. Center Masonite on linen, clip linen corners, and wrap over back of Masonite; fasten in place with artist's tape. Arrange pressed flowers on top of linen (we used lily of the valley at right; dogwood opposite). 3. Place linen-covered Masonite into frame so it faces up through the back of frame. Place glass on top. Glue moldings in place around inner sides of the frame; this holds glass in place and protects the frame from crumbs or spills. If you use an old frame—a favorite from home or a flea-market find, like the one on the opposite page— transforming it will be even easier since it's the detailed front of the frame that will be displayed. It won't require as many materials; just follow instructions above for attaching handles (in step one), then complete step two. Place glass and frame on top of linen, and secure frame back.

Fill pretty

packages

with the sweet

spirit of

the holiday

season

COOKIES
AND
CONFECTIONS

peppermint bark

marzipan snowmen

hazelnut brittle

icebox cookies

steamed pudding

Sweets are expected at the holidays, and making them to give as presents has always been one of the season's most enjoyable traditions. Fond memories of Christmas return as we stir a wintry brandy sauce or nibble on candy made but once a year. ✳ It's best to give cookies and candies that travel easily, don't need to be refrigerated, and can be neatly packaged into tins and boxes. Icebox cookies are indispensable for holiday planning. You can prepare the doughs up to three months ahead of time and freeze them. When you're ready to bake a fresh batch, take out one dough or several, slice off what you need, and return the rest to the freezer. ✳ Golden caramel is another perfect holiday treat, and making it is really quite simple. This melted-sugar concoction is as versatile today as it was around 800 A.D., when Arab confectioners named it *kurat al milh*, or "ball of sweet salt." Stir your favorite nuts into cooked caramel, and you have a wonderfully crunchy brittle. Or add heavy cream to hot caramel to make a delectable sauce for ice cream. ✳ As you choose your recipes, consider how you'll wrap the results. Devise a package that hints at what's inside: We placed peppermint bark made with crushed candy canes in red tins tied with red-and-white-striped ribbon. And don't forget that even the smallest gift can delight its recipient. Three little cookies in a pretty box can be the perfect surprise to leave on a colleague's desk or a loved one's pillow.

NUT CANDIES *Homemade candies made with fresh nuts (opposite) are packaged in tiny boxes tied with slender ribbon. Clockwise from left: Chocolate patties with chopped pistachios, bourbon pralines, turtles topped with crème caramel and chocolate, and caramelized almonds covered with cocoa powder and sugar. Most nuts are harvested in autumn and taste best around the holidays. Ask your grocer for the freshest ones available.*

PEPPERMINT BARK

MAKES 2¼ POUNDS OR ONE 11-BY-17-INCH SHEET

*If you don't have a double boiler, use a metal bowl set
over a pot of simmering water.*

  2 *pounds white chocolate, chopped
      into ½-inch pieces*
  12 *large candy canes*
  ½ *teaspoon peppermint oil*

1. Line an 11-by-17-inch baking sheet with parchment, and set aside.
2. In the top of a double boiler, melt the white chocolate, stirring constantly.
3. With a chef's knife or meat tenderizer, cut or pound candy into ¼-inch pieces.
4. Stir the pieces of candy canes and peppermint oil into the melted chocolate. Remove from heat, and pour the mixture onto the prepared baking sheet;

spread evenly. Chill until firm, 25 to 30 minutes. Break into pieces, and serve. Store in an airtight container in the refrigerator for up to 1 week.

CHOCOLATE-COVERED TURTLES

MAKES 55 TO 60

  1½ *pounds pecan halves (about 7½ cups)*
  1 *stick unsalted butter, cut up, plus
      more for pans*
  2 *cups light corn syrup*
  ½ *cup whole milk*
  2 *cups sugar*
     Pinch baking soda
  1 *twelve-ounce can evaporated milk*
  1 *pound semisweet chocolate*

1. Heat oven to 350°. Toast nuts on a baking pan for 10 minutes; remove from oven. Generously butter five baking pans. Arrange 5 pecan halves in a snowflake-shaped cluster, overlapping nuts in center. Repeat with remaining nuts; space clusters two inches apart.
2. In a heavy saucepan, combine corn syrup, whole milk, and sugar. Place over medium-high heat; cook, stirring occasionally with a wooden spoon, until syrup mixture comes to a boil, about 6 minutes. Stir in baking soda. Clip a candy thermometer to pan; add butter, stirring constantly until melted, keeping mixture at full boil. Slowly pour in evaporated milk; cook at a boil, stirring constantly, until temperature reaches 240° (soft-ball stage), about 45 minutes. If pan starts to overflow, turn down heat for a few minutes; return to a boil.
3. Remove caramel from heat; transfer to a medium metal bowl. Cool to 200°; caramel will have the consistency of thick honey.
4. Using a spoon, gently mound 1 tablespoon caramel on top of each cluster. Allow caramel to set up. If caramel becomes too stiff, place bowl over low heat; stir constantly for several minutes until returned to proper consistency.
5. Temper the chocolate following steps one through three in Chocolate-Nut Patties (recipe page 67).
6. Drizzle 1 tablespoon tempered chocolate over each cluster, and set aside in a cool place to harden. Store turtles in an airtight container at constant room temperature for up to 1 month.

CHOCOLATE-COVERED ALMONDS

MAKES ABOUT 2 POUNDS

2½ cups unblanched whole almonds (13 ounces)

1¼ cups granulated sugar

1 teaspoon ground cinnamon

1 pound semisweet chocolate, chopped

½ cup Dutch-process cocoa powder

½ cup confectioners' sugar

1. Heat oven to 350°. Toast almonds for 15 minutes on a baking sheet. Line two baking pans with parchment paper; set aside.

2. In a medium saucepan, combine the granulated sugar, ¼ cup water, toasted almonds, and cinnamon. Cook, stirring constantly, until the sugar becomes golden and granular and the almonds are completely coated and separated. Pour nuts onto prepared pans. Chill in freezer, about 15 minutes.

3. Meanwhile, place chocolate in a medium bowl; place bowl over simmering water until melted. Transfer half the chilled almonds to a large bowl, and pour half the melted chocolate over nuts. Stir until nuts are thoroughly coated. Transfer nuts onto prepared baking pan. Using two forks, separate nuts so none stick together. Return almonds to refrigerator until chocolate has set, about 20 minutes. Repeat with remaining almonds.

4. Place the cocoa powder and the confectioners' sugar into two separate bowls. Toss half the nuts in cocoa and half in sugar, and gently tap off any excess powder. Store the nuts separately in airtight containers for up to 1 month.

CHOCOLATE-NUT PATTIES

MAKES 30

1 pound semisweet chocolate

¾ cup assorted roasted and raw nuts, such as cashews, macadamias, pecans, walnuts, and hazelnuts, roughly chopped

1. To temper chocolate, cover a heating pad with a kitchen towel, and set pad to lowest setting. Line two baking pans with parchment paper, and set aside. Using a sharp knife, shave the chocolate.

2. In a medium glass bowl, heat two-thirds of the chocolate in microwave at 30 percent power for 1 minute. Stir chocolate; continue heating at 30 percent power in 10-second intervals until an instant-read thermometer registers 120°. Remove from microwave.

3. Stir in remaining shaved chocolate with rubber spatula. Stir constantly, bringing chocolate up sides and back down into bowl until temperature reaches between 86° and 89°. To determine if tempered, drizzle a thin line onto a cool stainless-steel surface. The chocolate should dry to a matte finish in about 5 minutes. Place bowl on covered heating pad; stir occasionally to maintain temperature between 86° and 89°, adjusting setting if necessary.

4. Working quickly, pour 2 tablespoons tempered chocolate onto prepared sheets to form 2-inch patties, spaced 2 inches apart. Let chocolate stand until it just begins to set. Sprinkle 1 teaspoon nuts in each center; set aside in a cool place to harden. Once completely set, transfer to an airtight container at constant room temperature for up to 1 month.

BOURBON PRALINES

MAKES ABOUT 18

1 cup nonfat buttermilk

1 teaspoon baking soda

2 cups sugar

5 tablespoons unsalted butter

1 tablespoon bourbon

1 cup pecan halves

1. Line two baking pans with parchment paper; set aside. In a 4-quart saucepan, add buttermilk, baking soda, and sugar. Over medium-high heat, bring to a rolling boil, stirring constantly. To prevent crystals from forming, brush sides of pan with cold water.

2. Cook, stirring constantly, until a candy thermometer registers 240° (soft-ball stage), about 15 minutes. Remove from heat. Add butter and bourbon; stir with a wooden spoon until butter melts. Stir in pecans; beat with wooden spoon for 30 seconds. Spoon 1 tablespoon of mixture onto prepared pan, forming a 2-inch patty. Repeat with remaining mixture. If mixture begins to harden, return to heat for 1 minute, scraping down sides and stirring. Let stand until set, about 1 hour. Refrigerate in an airtight container for up to 2 weeks.

PEPPERMINT BARK
Make a classic candy new with white chocolate, candy canes, and a few drops of natural peppermint oil (above). Line pink and red tins with parchment paper (opposite), stack the bark inside them, and wrap a pretty ribbon around each one. The airtight tins can be reused long after the candy disappears.

MARZIPAN SNOWMEN

The most unforgettable table settings often include something you can eat. Almond-flavored snowmen (this page) stand in a drift of sugar on an antique plate and make a lighthearted gift for guests to nibble for dessert.

CARAMEL BRITTLE

A stack of glistening nut brittle (opposite) shows off the array of textures and colors possible when clear amber caramel is mixed with various nuts and seeds. From top: sliced almonds, pumpkin seeds, sesame seeds, slivered almonds, pistachios, and hazelnuts.

MARZIPAN SNOWMEN

MAKES 8

You can find marzipan in specialty-food stores and many supermarkets.

- 1 *seven-ounce log marzipan*
  Food-coloring gel, in colors like red, green, and orange (see the Guide)
- 1 *cup superfine sugar*
  Toothpicks
  Fennel branches (see the Guide) or thin twigs

1. Divide marzipan into two equal pieces, reserving a ¾-inch-round ball of marzipan for "carrot" noses. To color marzipan, dip a toothpick into red food coloring; brush it on one half of marzipan. Knead the color into marzipan until it has spread evenly throughout, adding more color, a toothpickful at a time, until desired shade is reached. Repeat with second half of marzipan and green food coloring. From each colored half, roll out twelve ¾-inch-round balls (for snowmen bodies), and form 4 gumdrop-shaped hats. Reserve enough marzipan for 4 ropes; wrap one rope around the base of each hat for a brim.
2. Place sugar in a small bowl. Roll colored marzipan balls through sugar, a few at a time, lightly coating them. Using a toothpick as a "spine," skewer three same-colored marzipan balls on top of one another forming a snowman. Top each with a hat.
3. Attach the fennel-branch or twig arms to the middle ball of each snowman. Using a toothpick dabbed in food coloring, create the snowman's eyes.
4. Color reserved ball of marzipan with a toothpick dipped in orange food coloring until a carrotlike shade is reached. Form orange marzipan into small carrot-shaped noses; stick into place. Keep at room temperature in an airtight container up to 2 weeks (remove toothpick spine and twig arms before eating). Serve in a bed of "snow" (superfine sugar), if desired.

HAZELNUT BRITTLE

MAKES ONE 11-BY-17-INCH SHEET

To prevent crystallization, brush the sides of the saucepan with a pastry brush dipped in water as the caramel cooks.

- 4 *cups sugar*
- ¼ *teaspoon apple-cider vinegar*
- 5½ *cups hazelnuts*
  Vegetable oil, for pan and knife

1. Oil an 11-by-17-inch baking pan. Stir sugar, vinegar, and 1 cup water in a medium saucepan over medium heat until sugar dissolves. Cook without stirring until dark amber, 18 to 25 minutes. Stir in nuts.
2. Pour mixture onto pan. Let set until firm but still soft enough to cut. Unmold onto a cutting board. Working fast, use an oiled chef's knife to cut into six rectangles. Store in an airtight container up to 1 week.

CARAMEL-BOURBON-VANILLA SAUCE

MAKES 2 CUPS

- 2 *cups sugar*
- 1 *cup heavy cream*
- 1 *vanilla bean, split in half lengthwise*
- 2 *teaspoons freshly squeezed lemon juice*
- 2 *tablespoons unsalted butter*
- 1 *tablespoon bourbon*

1. Combine the sugar and ½ cup water in a 2-quart saucepan set over medium heat. Without stirring, cook mixture until dark amber in color, swirling the pan carefully while cooking, about 20 minutes.
2. Reduce the heat to low. Slowly add the cream, stirring with a wooden spoon. Scrape the vanilla seeds into the pan, and add the pod. Add the lemon juice, the butter, and the bourbon. Stir to combine.
3. Cover, and store, refrigerated, up to 1 week. Bring sauce to room temperature, or warm over low heat, before using.

LACY NUT COOKIES

MAKES ABOUT 4 DOZEN

- 1 *cup (2 sticks) plus 5 tablespoons unsalted butter*
- 2¼ *cups confectioners' sugar*
- ¼ *cup corn syrup*
- 1¼ *cups bread flour*
- 1¼ *cups chopped nuts, such as almonds, blanched hazelnuts, or pecans*

1. Heat oven to 350°. In the bowl of an electric mixer fitted with paddle attachment, cream the butter and sugar on medium speed until fluffy. With mixer running, add the corn syrup. Turn speed to low. Add flour; mix to combine. Add nuts; mix to combine.
2. Place a 12-by-16-inch piece of parchment on a work surface. Spoon dough across middle of parchment. Fold parchment over dough, and using a ruler, press

SNOWMEN TECHNIQUE
Our pastel snowmen (previous page) can be made quickly, so keep the ingredients on hand for when you need small gifts or favors. The technique is simple: Tint store-bought marzipan with food coloring, shape it into little balls, and roll them in superfine sugar. Stack three balls on toothpicks, and attach fennel branches or toothpicks for snowman arms.

and roll dough into a log. Chill at least 30 minutes.
3. Line two baking sheets with parchment. Remove parchment from log; slice into ½-inch-thick rounds. Place rounds on baking sheets, 3½ inches apart. Bake until golden brown and lacy, 15 to 20 minutes. Transfer to a wire rack to cool. Bake or freeze remaining dough. Store in an airtight container up to 2 weeks.

BLACK AND WHITE DOUGH
MAKES ABOUT 4 ¾ POUNDS

- 4 cups (8 sticks) unsalted butter, room temperature
- 1 teaspoon pure vanilla extract
- 3 cups confectioners' sugar
- 7½ cups bread flour
- ⅓ cup Dutch-process cocoa powder

1. To make white dough, place 2 cups butter, ½ teaspoon vanilla, 1½ cups sugar, and 3¾ cups flour in bowl of electric mixer fitted with paddle attachment. Mix on medium speed until well combined. Wrap in plastic.
2. To make chocolate dough, combine, in same bowl, remaining 2 cups butter, ½ teaspoon vanilla, 1½ cups sugar, 3¾ cups flour, and cocoa powder. Mix on medium speed until well combined. Wrap in plastic. Refrigerate up to 2 weeks, or freeze up to 3 months.

STRIPED BARS
MAKES ABOUT 6½ DOZEN

Black and White Dough (recipe above), room temperature

1. Divide chocolate dough into four equal pieces. Place between two 12-by-14-inch pieces of parchment. Roll into 3½-by-12-inch rectangles. Transfer to baking sheets. Chill 30 minutes. Repeat with white dough.
2. Remove top pieces of parchment from rectangles. Using bottom piece for support, invert one white rectangle onto a chocolate one, and remove parchment. Repeat, for a total of four layers. Wrap. Make a second brick with four remaining rectangles. Chill at least 1 hour.
3. Heat oven to 375°. Line two baking sheets with parchment paper. Unwrap the bricks, and trim evenly by ⅛ inch. Slice bricks into ¼-inch-thick rectangles, and place on sheets, spaced 2 inches apart.
4. Bake until just golden, 10 to 12 minutes. Transfer cookies to a wire rack to cool. Bake or freeze remaining dough. Store in an airtight container up to 2 weeks.

DESSERT SAUCE Caramel-bourbon-vanilla sauce (above) can top ice cream or fruit and is delectable enough to eat by the spoonful. Fill a humble jar with this velvety sauce, cover it with patterned paper and parchment for the lid, and it becomes a luxurious gift. Secure a small spoon to each one with butcher's twine for serving or for eating right out of the jar.

COOKIE SAMPLER *Boldly patterned icebox cookies make dramatic gifts in scallop-edged kraft-paper boxes embellished with decorative paper and ribbon. Clockwise from top left: Cornmeal-pecan biscuits, striped bars, lacy nut cookies, orange poppy-seed spirals, wheatmeal peanut-butter fingers, Neapolitan cookies (tied with ribbon), black-and-white bull's-eye cookies, and coconut-chocolate pinwheels (center).*

BULL'S-EYE COOKIES

MAKES ABOUT 7½ DOZEN

Black and White Dough (recipe page 71)

1. Place 20 ounces chocolate dough between two 12-by-14-inch pieces of parchment. Roll out to a 7-by-12 inch rectangle, about ⅓-inch thick. Repeat with 20 ounces white dough. Chill at least 30 minutes.

2. Place 12 ounces chocolate dough between two 12-by-14-inch pieces of parchment. Roll out to a 4¾-by-12-inch rectangle. Repeat with 12 ounces white dough. Chill both at least 15 minutes.

3. Place 6 ounces chocolate dough on a clean work surface. Roll into a 12-inch-long log, about ¾ inch in diameter. Repeat with 6 ounces white dough. Wrap in parchment. Chill both at least 15 minutes.

4. Remove top piece of parchment from the smaller chocolate rectangle. Unwrap white log, and place lengthwise on chocolate rectangle. Wrap chocolate dough around white log, pressing with fingers to seal seam. Roll log back and forth to smooth seam.

5. Repeat step four with the chocolate log and the smaller rectangle of white dough.

6. Remove top piece of parchment from the larger white rectangle. Place white log wrapped in chocolate dough lengthwise on the white rectangle. Wrap white dough around log, pressing with fingers to seal seam. Roll log back and forth to smooth seam.

7. Repeat step six with the chocolate log wrapped in white dough and the larger rectangle of chocolate dough. Wrap both logs in parchment. Chill 1 hour.

8. Heat oven to 375°. Line two baking sheets with parchment paper. Remove parchment from logs, and cut into ¼-inch-thick rounds; place on sheets, spaced 2 inches apart.

9. Bake the cookies until barely golden, about 15 minutes. Transfer the cookies to a wire rack to cool. Bake or freeze remaining dough. Store in an airtight container up to 2 weeks.

WHEATMEAL PEANUT-BUTTER FINGERS

MAKES ABOUT 3 DOZEN

- 1 cup butter (2 sticks), room temperature
- ¾ cup confectioners' sugar
- 1 large egg
- 1¼ cups toasted wheat germ
- 1¼ cups whole-grain pastry flour
- ¼ teaspoon salt
- ¼ cup cornstarch
- ¼ cup smooth peanut butter
- ¼ cup granulated sugar

1. Place the butter and confectioners' sugar in the bowl of an electric mixer fitted with the paddle attachment. Beat until fluffy, 2 to 3 minutes. Add the egg, and beat until fluffy.

2. In a medium bowl, whisk together the wheat germ, pastry flour, salt, and cornstarch. Add to the butter mixture, and beat on low speed until combined, about 1 minute.

3. Divide the dough into two equal parts, and place between 12-inch squares of parchment paper. Roll out each piece of dough into a 7-by-10-inch rectangle, about ¼-inch thick.

4. Remove the top pieces of parchment paper from the dough, and spread the peanut butter over one rectangle. Invert the second rectangle on top of the first. Folding any overhanging edges of parchment paper, wrap dough. Chill at least 1 hour.

5. Heat oven to 350°. Line two baking sheets with parchment. Unwrap dough. Generously sprinkle top and bottom with sugar. Trim edges, creating a clean rectangle. Cut into three dozen 3½-by-½-inch rectangles; place on sheets, spaced 1½ inches apart.

6. Bake the cookies until barely golden, about 22 minutes. Transfer to a wire rack to cool. Bake or freeze the remaining dough. Store in an airtight container up to 2 weeks.

COOKIE TECHNIQUES

1. Striped cookies are made by slicing a slab of layered black and white dough. 2. For bull's-eye cookies, wrap a narrow log of dough in two concentric layers of alternating black and white doughs. Upon slicing, each cookie will resemble a bull's eye. 3. To make wheatmeal peanut-butter fingers, spread smooth peanut butter over a layer of dough; top with a second layer of dough, then chill. Sprinkle with granulated sugar before slicing to give each cookie a sparkly, crunchy top.

COCONUT-CHOCOLATE PINWHEELS

MAKES ABOUT 3 DOZEN

White cookie dough studded with shredded coconut is wrapped around bittersweet chocolate in these rich, creamy cookies.

     9 tablespoons unsalted butter, room temperature
     1 cup sugar
     1 large egg
     1 teaspoon pure vanilla extract
     2 cups cake flour (not self-rising)
     ½ teaspoon baking soda
     ¼ teaspoon salt
     1½ cups shredded unsweetened coconut
     6 ounces bittersweet chocolate, chopped
     ⅓ cup sweetened condensed milk

1. In the bowl of an electric mixer fitted with the paddle attachment, combine 8 tablespoons butter and the sugar, and cream together until fluffy. Add the egg and the vanilla, and beat until fluffy.
2. In a medium bowl, whisk together the flour, baking soda, and salt. Add the flour mixture to the butter mixture, and beat on low speed until combined. Add the coconut, and beat until combined. Place the dough between two 12-by-17-inch pieces of parchment paper, and roll out into a 10-by-15-inch rectangle, about ⅛-inch thick. Transfer the dough in the parchment paper to a baking sheet, and chill at least 1 hour.
3. Place the chocolate and the remaining tablespoon butter in the top of a double boiler or a heatproof bowl set over a pan of simmering water. Melt completely, about 2 minutes, and remove from heat. Stir in the condensed milk. Let sit until slightly thickened, about 5 minutes.
4. Remove the dough from the refrigerator. Peel off the top piece of parchment paper. Using an offset spatula, spread the melted-chocolate mixture over the dough. Using the bottom piece of parchment paper for support, roll the dough into a log. Wrap the log in parchment, and chill overnight.
5. Heat oven to 350°. Line two baking sheets with parchment paper. Remove the parchment from the log, and cut the log into ¼-inch-thick rounds. Place the rounds on the baking sheets, spaced about 1½ inches apart. Bake the cookies until pale golden brown around the edges, 8 to 10 minutes. Transfer the cookies to a wire rack to cool. Bake or freeze the remaining dough. Store the cookies in an airtight container up to 2 weeks.

CORNMEAL-PECAN BISCUITS

MAKES 2½ DOZEN

     ½ cup whole pecans
     8 tablespoons (1 stick) unsalted butter
     1 cup sugar
     1 large egg
     1 teaspoon pure vanilla extract
     1¼ cups all-purpose flour
     ½ cup yellow cornmeal
     1 teaspoon baking powder
     ¼ teaspoon salt
     1 teaspoon ground cinnamon
     2 tablespoons packed dark-brown sugar
     1 large egg white, lightly beaten with 1
       tablespoon water

1. Heat oven to 400°. Place the pecans on a baking sheet. Toast in oven until golden and fragrant, 8 to 10 minutes. Let pecans cool.
2. In the bowl of an electric mixer fitted with the paddle attachment, cream the butter and sugar on medium speed until light and fluffy, 2 to 4 minutes. Add the egg and vanilla; incorporate.
3. In a medium bowl, whisk together the flour, cornmeal, baking powder, and salt. On low speed, add the flour mixture to the butter mixture. Mix until combined, about 30 seconds.
4. Transfer the dough to a clean work surface, and divide into four equal portions. Place one portion between two 12-inch-square pieces of parchment paper. Roll out dough to a 3½-by-9-inch rectangle. Repeat with the three remaining portions dough. Transfer to baking sheets; chill at least 10 minutes.
5. In the bowl of a food processor, process the pecans, cinnamon, and brown sugar until the nuts have been finely chopped, 12 to 15 seconds. Transfer the mixture to a medium bowl.
6. Remove top pieces of parchment from dough. Brush one lightly with egg white; sprinkle ¼ cup pecan mixture over top. Brush second rectangle lightly with egg wash. Invert second rectangle over first; remove parchment on top. Repeat layering process, leaving top rectangle uncoated. Trim to a 3¼-by-8½-inch brick. Wrap, and chill overnight.
7. Heat oven to 350°. Line two baking sheets with parchment. Cut the brick into ¼-inch-thick rectangles, and transfer to baking sheets, 2½ inches apart.
8. Bake until light golden, 12 to 15 minutes. Transfer to a wire rack to cool. Bake or freeze remaining dough. Store in an airtight container up to 2 weeks.

ICEBOX-COOKIE DOUGH
Fill your freezer with gifts: Bundle logs with brightly colored ribbon (above) to give to holiday hosts and unexpected guests. Using a ruler to shape the dough into neat logs (top), wrap the dough in parchment paper, and label each log. Twist the ends tightly, and store the logs in the freezer. Be sure to include baking instructions or the recipe on a card.

NEAPOLITAN COOKIES

MAKES ABOUT 8 DOZEN

This dough is cut into bricks, much like the ice cream that inspired its name.

  1 cup dried cranberries, roughly chopped
     Orange-Sablé Dough (recipe page 77),
     room temperature
  1 cup walnuts, coarsely chopped
     Chocolate-Espresso Dough (recipe page 77),
     room temperature

1. Line an 8-inch-square baking pan with plastic. In a large bowl, stir cranberries into orange-sablé dough. In another large bowl, stir walnuts into chocolate-espresso dough.
2. Press orange mixture into bottom of pan. Using an offset spatula, smooth top evenly. Spread chocolate mixture over orange mixture, and smooth evenly. Cover pan with plastic. Chill at least 2 hours.
3. Heat oven to 350°. Line two baking sheets with parchment paper. Unmold dough; remove plastic. Cut into 2-by-8-inch bricks; cut bricks into ¼-inch-thick slices. Place slices on sheets, spaced 1½ inches apart. Bake until firm to the touch, 12 to 15 minutes. Transfer cookies to a wire rack to cool. Bake or freeze remaining dough. Store in an airtight container up to 2 weeks.

ORANGE POPPY-SEED SPIRALS

MAKES ABOUT 3 DOZEN

     Orange-Sablé Dough (recipe page 77)
  ⅓ cup poppy seeds

1. Bring dough to room temperature. Place between two 12-by-14-inch pieces of parchment paper; roll out to an 8-by-12-inch rectangle. Transfer to a baking sheet; chill 30 minutes.
2. Transfer dough to a clean work surface. Remove top piece of parchment; sprinkle poppy seeds over top. Using bottom parchment to support dough, fold bottom edge to meet middle. Fold over two more times, forming a 1-inch-tall rectangle. Wrap; chill at least 2 hours.
3. Heat oven to 350°. Line two baking sheets with parchment. Remove parchment from dough, and cut into ¼-inch-thick squares. Place on baking sheets, spaced 2 inches apart.
4. Bake cookies until edges turn light golden, about 15 minutes. Transfer to a wire rack to cool. Bake or freeze remaining dough. Store in an airtight container up to 2 weeks.

ORANGE-GINGER ROUNDS

MAKES ABOUT 5 DOZEN

Chill this soft dough a bit longer than the other versions so it holds its shape when rolled in the ginger.

     Orange-Sablé Dough (recipe page 77)
  6 ounces crystallized ginger (see the Guide),
     finely chopped, about 1 cup

1. Place two 12-by-16-inch pieces of parchment on a work surface. Divide dough in half; form each half into a rough log on parchment. Fold parchment over dough; using a ruler, roll and press dough into a 1½-inch cylinder. Wrap. Chill at least 3 hours.
2. Heat oven to 350°. Line two baking sheets with parchment. Spread crystallized ginger on a work surface. Unwrap logs; roll in ginger to coat. Cut logs into ¼-inch-thick rounds; place on sheets, spaced 2 inches apart. Bake until edges turn slightly golden, about 15 minutes. Transfer cookies to a wire rack to cool. Bake or freeze remaining dough. Store in an airtight container up to 2 weeks.

COOKIE TECHNIQUES

1. Coconut-chocolate pinwheels get their shape when ganache, spread over coconut cookie dough, is rolled into a log. 2. Cornmeal pecan biscuits are made by sprinkling pecans, brown sugar, and cinnamon between layers of cornmeal cookie dough. 3. The chocolate-espresso layer and orange-sablé-dough layer of these Neapolitan cookies are stacked, chilled, then cut. 4. Orange-sablé dough is rolled in crystallized ginger, forming delicious edges around the cookies.

ORANGE-SABLE DOUGH

MAKES ABOUT 1½ POUNDS

"Sablé" is the French word for "sandy." This classic dough produces cookies with a remarkably delicate texture—they crumble the minute they're in your mouth.

- 1¼ cups whole blanched almonds
- 1 cup confectioners' sugar
- ¾ cup (1½ sticks) unsalted butter
- 3 tablespoons finely grated orange zest (2 to 3 oranges)
- 1 large egg
- 1 tablespoon freshly squeezed lemon juice
- 1½ cups all-purpose flour

1. Place the almonds and sugar in the bowl of a food processor. Process until the mixture resembles coarse cornmeal, and set aside.

2. Place the butter and orange zest in the bowl of an electric mixer fitted with the paddle attachment. Beat on medium speed until white and fluffy, 2 to 3 minutes. On low speed, add the almond mixture, and beat until combined, 10 to 15 seconds. Add the egg and lemon juice, and combine. Add the flour, and beat until combined. Wrap in plastic; store, refrigerated, up to 1 week, or freeze up to 3 months.

CHOCOLATE WAFERS

MAKES ABOUT 6 DOZEN

Always a Christmas classic, chocolate wafers are delicious eaten straight from the wrapping or sandwiched around a scoop of ice cream.

Chocolate-Espresso Dough (recipe follows), room temperature

1. Place a 12-by-16-inch piece of parchment paper on a clean work surface. Spoon the dough down the center of the parchment paper. Fold the parchment paper over the dough. Using a ruler, roll and press the dough into a tight log. Wrap the dough in another layer of parchment paper, and chill at least 1 hour.

2. Heat oven to 350°. Line two baking sheets with parchment paper. Unwrap the log, and slice into ⅛-inch-thick rounds. Place the rounds on baking sheets, spaced about 1½ inches apart.

3. Bake the wafers until firm to the touch, 20 to 25 minutes. Transfer the wafers to a wire rack to cool. Bake or freeze the remaining dough. Store in an airtight container at room temperature up to 2 weeks.

CHOCOLATE-ESPRESSO DOUGH

MAKES 19 OUNCES

If you grind your own espresso beans, be sure to grind them to a superfine powder.

- 1½ cups all-purpose flour
- ½ cup Dutch-process cocoa powder
- ½ tablespoon finely ground espresso beans
- 1 cup (2 sticks) unsalted butter, room temperature
- 1 cup confectioners' sugar
- 1 teaspoon pure vanilla extract

1. In a large bowl, sift together flour, cocoa powder, and espresso beans; set aside.

2. In the bowl of an electric mixer fitted with the paddle attachment, combine butter, sugar, and vanilla until creamy, 3 to 4 minutes. Working in additions, gradually beat in flour mixture, scraping down sides of bowl twice. Wrap in plastic; store, refrigerated, up to 2 weeks, or freeze up to 3 months.

BRANDY SAUCE

MAKES 1 CUP

Brandy sauce is similar to the other popular steamed pudding accompaniment, hard sauce. They're both stiff sauces that are served chilled with the warm puddings.

- 2 large egg yolks
- ½ cup heavy cream
- 4 tablespoons unsalted butter, room temperature, cut in pieces
- ½ cup sugar
- 2 tablespoons cognac

1. Combine water and ice in a medium bowl for an ice bath, and set aside. In a medium bowl, lightly beat the egg yolks.

2. In a small, heavy saucepan, bring the cream to a boil over medium-high heat. Stir in the butter and sugar, and stir until completely dissolved, about 2 minutes. Whisk about a fourth of the cream mixture into the egg yolks, whisking constantly to prevent curdling. Transfer egg-yolk mixture back to the saucepan and bring to a boil, whisking constantly. Reduce heat and simmer, whisking frequently, until mixture is very thick, about 5 minutes. (Mixture will have the consistency of a thick pudding.) Remove from heat, and stir in cognac. Transfer sauce to a clean bowl and place in ice bath to chill. Brandy sauce will keep in the refrigerator, in an airtight container, for 1 week.

COOKIE ROLLS *When icebox cookies are this pretty (opposite), why hide them? Stack alternating layers of chocolate wafers and orange-ginger rounds, or make a stack of one type of cookie. Wrap them in clear cellophane for a dramatic effect. Tie the ends securely with ribbon to keep the cookies fresh for the holidays.*

FIG OR APRICOT STEAMED PUDDINGS

This pudding may be made with figs for a dark, rich, traditional pudding, or with dried apricots for a lighter, slightly tarter version. Whole or halved dried apricots may be used. You'll need eight small pudding molds (see the Guide). Steam for 2 hours to produce moister puddings, 2 hours 20 minutes for denser puddings.

- 1½ pounds (about 84) stemmed dried Black Mission figs (see the Guide) to make about 4 cups or 2 pounds dried whole or halved apricots to make about 4 cups
- ½ cup brandy
- 1 cup (2 sticks) unsalted butter, at room temperature, plus 2 tablespoons, melted, for buttering molds
- 2 cups packed dark-brown sugar
- 4 large eggs
- 1 teaspoon pure vanilla extract
- 3 cups all-purpose flour
- 1 tablespoon baking powder
- ½ teaspoon salt
- 1 teaspoon ground cinnamon
- ¼ teaspoon ground cardamom
- 2 cups milk
- ½ cup apricot jam
- Brandy Sauce (recipe page 77)

PUDDING FOR ONE

Christmas without pudding is like a birthday without cake. These sweet desserts-for-one are flavored with dried apricots or figs and served with brandy sauce on antique Steuben swirled-glass plates (above). To ensure their safe and memorable arrival, leave the puddings in their molds, and pour the sauce into small lidded tins (opposite) adorned with satin or flocked-paper lids, satin ribbons, and metallic-silver tassels and beads.

1. In a large saucepan over medium-high heat, combine 2 cups figs (or apricots), 1 cup water, and the brandy; bring to a boil. Reduce heat to low, and simmer for about 5 minutes, just until figs are plumped (there should still be 1 cup liquid in the pan). Transfer the mixture, with all the liquid, to a food processor, and process until puréed. Set aside.

2. Place remaining figs in a small bowl. Cover with boiling water, and let soak until fruit is plump, about 10 minutes. Drain thoroughly, and set aside.

3. Using a pastry brush, butter eight 2- or 3-cup pudding molds and their lids (or use eight circles of parchment paper cut several inches larger than mold for lids). Set aside.

4. In the bowl of an electric mixer, beat together butter and sugar on medium speed until softened and well combined, 3 to 4 minutes. Add eggs, one at a time, and continue beating until each is incorporated. Add vanilla and reserved fig purée, and beat until combined, about 1 minute.

5. In a large bowl, sift together flour, baking powder, salt, cinnamon, and cardamom. Set the mixer to low speed, and gradually add the flour mixture, alternating with the milk, to the fig mixture, in two additions each. Beat until well combined, about 2 minutes, scraping down the sides of the bowl as necessary.

6. Place jam in a small saucepan and heat, stirring, over medium heat just until warm. Spoon about 1 tablespoon warm jam into bottom of each pudding mold. Cut the reserved figs in half lengthwise, and arrange 8 to 10 halves cut-sides up, on the bottoms of each of the molds, overlapping slightly. (Dried apricots do not need to be cut. Arrange 8 to 10 as above in the bottom of each mold.) Pour 1 cup batter into each mold. Tap molds sharply on counter several times to distribute batter evenly and to eliminate air bubbles. Cover each mold with its lids or parchment paper secured with a rubber band. (If using parchment, place a layer of aluminum foil on top of the paper to prevent water from coming in contact with the puddings.) Puddings may be made up to this point and refrigerated for 1 day. (If refrigerated, leave puddings at room temperature for 1 hour before steaming.)

7. To steam the puddings, place a 10-inch round rack in the bottom of an 8- to 10-quart stockpot; place three or four molds (depending on the size of the molds, either three or four will fit at one time) on the rack. Remaining puddings may sit at room temperature or be refrigerated for about 45 minutes while others are steaming. (Do not refrigerate puddings the entire steaming time, or they will be too cold to cook properly.) Pour enough boiling water into the pot to reach halfway up the sides of molds. Cover, and bring to boil over high heat. Reduce heat to medium low, and gently steam puddings until a toothpick inserted in the middles comes out clean, 2 hours to 2 hours 20 minutes. Transfer molds to a cooling rack; when cool enough to handle, remove lids. Let sit, uncovered, for about 5 minutes for puddings; turn out onto serving plates. Serve warm with chilled brandy sauce.

TO REWARM FIG OR APRICOT PUDDINGS: Heat oven to 350°. Transfer puddings from refrigerator to a rimmed baking sheet. Keep puddings in molds with their lids. Place in oven. Heat for 40 minutes or until a metal skewer inserted into pudding comes out very hot to the touch. Using a pot holder or kitchen towel, carefully unmold puddings onto serving plates. Serve warm with brandy sauce.

Create many gifts
quickly using
the same method,
then make each
one a bit different

GIFTS FOR
A LONG,
LONG LIST

hot chocolate recipe ~

snow globes

ribbon bookmarks

shell candles

Mexican hot chocolate

organza sachets

Old neighbors and new acquaintances, the children's teachers and coaches, your colleagues and cousins—the number of people who ought to get a personal gift grows every year. But when your holiday list starts to curl like Santa's fabled scroll, it's time to take a couple of lessons from the old boy himself: Start a workshop and stay merry. ✳ In fact, the two notions go together very well. A clever gift idea and a well-organized assembly line can provide many hours of fun and a host of creative pleasures. And, as you will find with the projects here, after the making, there's the immense satisfaction of crossing all the names off your list without undue toil or expenditure as well as the particular pride that comes from giving presents loaded with handmade charm and lots of personal touches. ✳ The first stage and creative opportunity in giving these gifts is gathering the simple materials that will be assembled. You can complete this step well in advance, making your holiday weeks much less hectic. For some of these gifts, in fact, you will probably make your best discoveries at unexpected times throughout the year. You might get an inspirational burst of holiday spirit, for example, strolling along a beach in August, finding the perfect shells for holding colored candles peeking out of the sand. At the flea markets on a spring or fall weekend, you might discover just the right kind of café au lait bowls in which to assemble kits for heavenly hot

MEXICAN HOT CHOCOLATE
A cup is nice, but a bowl is better. Assemble the ingredients for making perfect hot chocolate in bowls big enough to thrill serious chocolate lovers (opposite). Buy Mexican chocolate, cinnamon sticks, vanilla beans, and mini marshmallows in quantity; package enough of each to fill a café au lait bowl with steaming hot chocolate. Include a recipe (see page 87), and tie it all together with ribbon.

chocolate. And a stop at a hobby shop will turn up all manner of figurines to put into snow globes. You should also be saving your good jars and lids all year long for these simple keepsakes, stored in a box ready for your "workshop." ✳ Most of the bulk ingredients and the containers for our prettily repackaged food gifts can also be

gathered at your convenience and quickly put together when gift-giving time arrives. With some empty cookie tins, big bags of chamomile and rose hips, and a bowl of homemade sugar stars, you can compose a stack of lovely herbal-tea sets in minutes. Or buy jars of lemon curd and lime and orange marmalade well ahead of time, make a pile of pomander balls on a

winter day, then simply tie them all together for a fragrant and delicious citrus gift. ✳ You will find the sewn gifts presented in this chapter just as easy to make, whether you assemble ribbon bookmarks, herbal organza sachets, or elegant satin and felt pouches for compact discs and notebooks. Collect all your fabrics and ribbons, cut multiple swatches and lengths to the pattern, then weave or sew them together with custom touches for each recipient. Even the simplest of all the gifts here, ribbon-wrapped candles, can be customized to give your friends the colors and shapes they like best.

FABRIC ENVELOPES
Well-chosen compact discs are always appreciated. Make giving them more personal by slipping the CDs into delightful hand-stitched pouches made from felt or wide ribbon, secured with narrow or wide ribbons (left and opposite). The envelopes can be used over and over, as sachets or filled with travel toiletries. You can also vary the size and shape of the envelopes, to fit blank books, pencils, diaries, or eyeglasses. For instructions, see page 86.

JARS, TINS, AND BOXES
Handcrafting snow globes
allows you to create wintry
scenes using figurines, glitter,
and small kitchen jars (below).
For instructions, see page 86.
Give packaged-food gifts a
homemade touch by assembling
and wrapping them yourself.
Opposite, clockwise from top
left: Wrapping corrugated
paper trimmed with grosgrain
ribbon around a fruit crate
makes a beautiful gift box for
clementines, chestnuts, and

hazelnuts. A band of corrugated
paper turns the inside of
store-bought tins into sectioned
boxes for loose teas and sugar
stars and snowflakes (recipe,
page 87). Pecans, raisins, and
crystallized ginger are neatly
arranged in a woven box,
embellished with a walnut
glued to ribbon; the ribbon
snippet is attached with a
pearl-head pin. Citrus fruit
dotted with cloves hint at the
orange and lime marmalade
and lemon curd inside the jars.

PACKAGING GIFTS ASSEMBLY-LINE STYLE

CD pouches, snow globes, clementine boxes, and ribbon bookmarks

CD POUCHES These pouches can be made out of wide ribbon or felt (bottom left and page 83). For ribbon, cut a piece 5 by 17 inches. Stitch a line across bottom of ribbon to prevent fraying. For felt, cut a piece 5½ by 17½ inches, and trim edges with pinking shears. With right sides together, fold fabric 5 inches from the bottom. Pin each side; stitch. Press seams open; turn right side out. Place CD inside; fold top flap over. Tie a wide satin ribbon into a bow or a velvet ribbon into a knot. Or tie two narrow ribbons into bows, using tweezers to make crisp loops.

SNOW GLOBES Baby-food, pimiento, and olive jars are good for making these globes (bottom right and page 85). Look for plastic or ceramic figurines (metal are prone to rust) at flea markets and hobby shops. Synthetic evergreen tips are available at many floral-supply stores. If the colors of the jar lids are not seasonal, paint them with oil-based enamel paint. Sand inside of jar lid until surface is rough. With clear-drying epoxy, adhere figurine and evergreen to inside of lid; let epoxy dry. Fill jar almost to top with distilled water; add a pinch of glitter and a dash of glycerin (available at drugstores) to keep glitter from falling too quickly. Don't add too much or glitter will stick to bottom of jar when flipped. Gently screw on lid, being careful not to dislodge figurine. Shake, and enjoy.

CLEMENTINE BOXES To make the box on page 84, you'll need a produce shipping crate, a utility knife, corrugated paper, a bone folder (available at art-supply stores), craft glue, and narrow grosgrain ribbon. Cut a piece of rectangular corrugated paper 2½ times the length of bottom and sides of box. Center box on paper. Fold along the height; score folds with bone folder for crisp edges. **1.** Cut a second piece of corrugated paper 2½ times the width and height of sides. Center box on paper. Fold along height; score folds. Using the ruler and utility knife, trim the four corners of this paper on an angle from edge to fold. Center the trimmed paper on rectangular paper, place box in center, and fold rectangular paper over top of box to create flaps. **2.** Fold angled flaps over, brush edges with glue, and, beginning on bottom of box, trim with ribbon (left).

RIBBON BOOKMARKS To make this bookmark (opposite page and page 90), you'll need two ribbons of different widths and textures (we used grosgrain, satin, and velvet; grosgrain doesn't fray), scissors, a ruler, a utility knife, and needle and thread. Cut ribbons to desired length (ours are 14 and 16 inches long and 1½ and 2¼ inches wide); thinner ribbon will be on top of wider ribbon. Measure width of thin ribbon to determine location and width of slits on wide ribbon. On wrong side of wide ribbon, make evenly spaced pencil lines along its length where each slit should be, using a ruler. Carefully cut each slit along edge of ruler with utility knife. Weave thin ribbon through slits on wide ribbon. To hold in place, stitch straight across top and bottom of ribbons. Fringe ends or adorn with a button, bell, or charm.

MEXICAN HOT CHOCOLATE

MAKES 4 SIX-OUNCE SERVINGS

Mexican chocolate is a flavorful combination of choco-late, cinnamon, almonds, and sugar. There are many brands available, some sweeter than others. A bag of sugar cubes may be included in your gift for those who like their chocolate even sweeter.

3½ ounces sweet Mexican chocolate,
    roughly chopped
3 cups milk
½ vanilla bean, split in half lengthwise
    (optional)
4 cinnamon sticks, for stirrers (optional)

1. In a medium saucepan, combine chocolate with 3 tablespoons water over medium heat. Using the back of a fork, mash the chocolate into the water, and stir until the chocolate is melted and smooth and begins to bubble around the edges, about 2 minutes.
2. Add the milk and vanilla bean, if using, to the saucepan, and heat, stirring occasionally, until wisps of steam begin to rise from the surface of the milk; don't let milk come to a boil. Transfer from heat. Remove the vanilla bean. To make hot choco-late frothy, carefully transfer it to a blender, and blend until foamy. Divide the hot chocolate evenly between 4 mugs. Garnish each mug with a cinna-mon-stick stirrer, if desired, and serve right away.

SUGAR STARS AND SNOWFLAKES

MAKES 7½ DOZEN STARS AND 11 DOZEN
SNOWFLAKES

Plastic molds are used to transform loose sugar into crisp decorative shapes. The sugar may be used white or tint it with very strongly brewed tea. (Black tea should be brewed until very dark.) To order plastic molds, see the Guide.

1 one-pound box superfine sugar
5 teaspoons water or strongly brewed tea

1. Line a work surface with parchment paper.
2. On a separate work surface, combine the sugar with the water or tea in a medium bowl. Using your hands, work the water into the sugar until it is the consistency of wet sand; the sugar should hold its shape when squeezed together in your hand.
3. Using your fingertips, press small amounts of the sugar mixture tightly into the plastic molds. Scrape the excess sugar back into the bowl, using the side of a metal spatula or the back of a knife. Use your fin-gertips again to tightly pack the sugar into each in-dividual mold. Carefully invert the filled molds onto the parchment-lined surface. Gently tap the molds to release the shapes onto the parchment pa-per. Carefully lift off molds. (Make 5 sheets of the star molds and 5 sheets of the snowflake molds, to yield a total of 10 sheets of sugar shapes.) Allow the shapes to sit at room temperature until completely dry and hard, about 1 hour 15 minutes. When the shapes are ready, the surface feels firm to the touch and should not give when lightly pressed with your finger. Store in an airtight container, at room tem-perature, for up to 2 months.

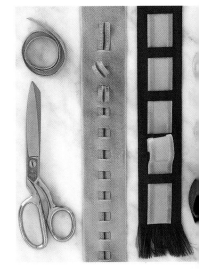

BOOKMARK TECHNIQUE
Cut lengths of ribbon of different widths and textures sized to the book they will be used in. With a utility knife, make evenly spaced slits along the length of the wider ribbon. Weave the narrow ribbon through the slits, and stitch it in place at the top and bottom of the bookmark. See page 86 for more instruc-tions. Additional bookmarks are also pictured on page 90.

SHELL CANDLES *Brighten a winter table with memories of summer. The shells the ocean cast at your feet last summer make lovely gifts with candles formed inside them. Deep shells like scallops and clams work best and burn longest. Clean the shells in a weak solution of bleach and water; let dry. Melt paraffin wax or existing candles in the top of a double boiler. We mixed the melted wax of pink, mauve, and yellow candles to create coral tones that complement our shells. Cut wicking to two to three inches, and attach to a metal wick holder (opposite, top left); set aside. Pour melted wax into shell. Place wick and holder in bottom of shell. If wick droops, trim. Let cool until hardened, about 30 minutes. If a shell wobbles, stabilize it by resting it on the top of a cup.*

STACKED ORGANZA SACHETS *Tie together three or four of these organza pouches filled with moth-repellent herbs (above) to make pretty, practical gifts, and a sweet-smelling alternative to mothballs. Sachets can be stored with wool clothing, but woolens must be dry cleaned first; it is actually the oils on unclean clothing that attract moths. Cut two 4½-inch-squares of organza. Place squares on top of one another, and pin together (above left). Sew three sides with a tight zigzag stitch, leaving a 1-inch seam allowance. Mix two parts lavender, wormwood, cedar, or patchouli with one part rosemary, tansy, cinnamon, or cloves (the last four herbs have weaker moth-repellent qualities, but add a pleasing scent). Funnel the mixture into the organza pouch, and sew the remaining side. Trim the edges with scalloped scissors.*

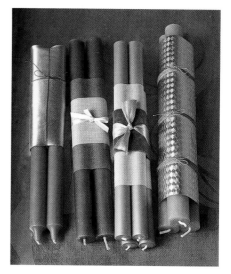

CANDLE SETS *Wrapped in colorful or white paper bands and satin bows, candles are almost too pretty to light. To give round or square pillar candles (opposite), wrap a wide band of linen-patterned glassine around one, two, or three candles, and secure a box of matches to the package with narrow ribbon, finished in a tight knot. Instead of a card, wrap the matchbox in decorative paper stamped with a greeting. Tapers lend themselves to a host of creative wrapping ideas (above). Don't throw away scraps of favorite ribbons or papers; make a single band or layer one on top of another to bundle like-colored candles. Tie with a satin ribbon—or three.*

RIBBON BOOKMARKS *Personalize a thoughtfully chosen book with a bookmark you made yourself. To create a fringed edge, stitch across the bottom of the bookmark, about $1/2$ inch from the bottom. Pull away the threads running crosswise. See page 86 for full instructions. Above, left to right: The gold velvet ribbon is threaded through with two slender ribbons of different textures and finished with a tiny button. A felt star, a star-shaped button, and a tiny bead anchor a grosgrain bookmark. A velvet-bordered pink satin ribbon, woven along a chocolate ribbon, is embellished with pink buttons. The ends of a 2-inch-wide piece of elastic that has been dyed are stitched together to form a loop; the holly-leaf decoration is cut from silver grosgrain ribbon. Sometimes a piece of ribbon, like the braided one, is so pretty it needs no adornment.*

Hors d'oeuvres
are spiced
for the season
and packed for
tempting
presentation

SAVORIES
FOR GIFTS
AND
GATHERINGS

Olives scented with citrus and rosemary, nuts crusted with allspice and cumin, flaky puff-pastry straws: Pack our homemade treats in a bowl or basket, wrap it, and you will have a practical and memorable gift that's ready to serve, which means less work for the busy host. And when the food has disappeared, the container will serve as a reminder of your culinary skill and thoughtfulness. ✳ Our savories and the charming ways they're presented have a global flavor. Mediterranean-style olives, goat-cheese spread, and assorted crackers are packed in a Japanese bento box. Prosciutto bread, a savory version of the traditional sweet yeast bread from

Verona, is displayed in a distinctive star-shaped mold. From our own shores, the native American cranberry has become a holiday staple. Cranberry chutney makes a versatile gift, preserved in ribbon-wrapped canning jars. ✳ Almost all the recipes here will make a large batch of savories that will keep through weeks of party giving. With plenty on hand, last-minute gifts are easy to assemble.

BENTO BOXES *Double-decker Japanese lunch boxes (opposite, see the Guide) provide elegant packaging and transportation for (top, clockwise from top) caraway-onion cards, simple white crackers, sweet-potato chips, phyllo knots, and cheese and poppy-seed straws, and for (bottom, clockwise from top) spiced nuts, citrus and rosemary olives, and herbed goat cheese. Trim the boxes with varying widths of velvet, satin, and silk ribbon (above).*

CRANBERRY CHUTNEY *Swags of red satin ribbon cinched with vintage gold ribbon (above left) turn a practical present into a gorgeous gift. Jewel-toned chutney packed in glass canning jars is pretty unadorned, but a satin-covered lid and handmade label (above center) or three strands of ribbon (above right) make it dressed for the occasion. Food packaged in these jars must be refrigerated.*

CRANBERRY CHUTNEY

MAKES 6 HALF-PINT JARS

- ½ cup apple-cider vinegar
- ⅔ cup packed light-brown sugar
- 1 teaspoon salt
- ½ teaspoon ground cardamom
- 1 cup candied orange peel, cut into ¼-inch pieces
- ½ cup finely diced celery (2 to 3 ribs)
- 1½ cups finely diced red onion (1 medium red onion)
- 2 apples, peeled, cored, and cut into ¼-inch cubes
- 5 cups whole frozen cranberries

1. Combine vinegar, sugar, salt, cardamom, orange peel, celery, red onion, apples, and 2 cups water in a shallow 6-quart saucepan. Set over medium-high heat; bring to a boil, stirring occasionally.

2. Reduce heat to medium, and simmer until the apples are tender and most of the liquid has been absorbed, 30 to 40 minutes.

3. Stir in cranberries, and cook until they begin to pop, 10 to 15 minutes. Remove from heat.

4. Transfer chutney immediately to jars as directed in "Canning Tips," below. Alternatively, transfer to a large bowl set over an ice bath to chill; store in airtight container, refrigerated, up to 4 weeks.

CANNING TIPS Chutneys can be made and eaten right away or stored in the refrigerator for several weeks, but if you plan to give them as gifts, the only safe way to keep them is to follow these canning instructions. The United States Department of Agriculture offers a complete guide to home canning, which can be found on the Internet. See www.foodsafety.org/canhome.htm.

1. Discard any jars that have chips or cracks. Wash the jars, lids, and screw bands in hot, soapy water; rinse well. Place jars upright on a wire rack placed in a large pot, leaving at least an inch of space between jars. Fill with hot water until the jars are submerged, and bring to a boil. Boil for 15 minutes. Turn off heat; leave the jars in the water. Sterilize the lids according to manufacturer's instructions. Never reuse lids—the seals may not work a second time.

2. Using a jar lifter and tongs, lift the jars from the pot, emptying the water back into the pot, and place the jars on a layer of clean towels. Place a stainless-steel canning funnel in the mouth of a jar, and fill with hot chutney to a quarter inch from the rim. Remove the funnel, and run a small rubber spatula around the edges to release excess air bubbles. Clean the rim and threads of the jar with a clean towel dipped in hot water. Use tongs to lift a prepared lid, and place it carefully on the rim of the jar. Screw on the band until it is secure but not too tight, or the air in the jars will not be able to escape and the jars will not be properly sealed.

3. After each jar is filled, place it back into the pot of water. When all of the jars have been returned to the pot, cover and bring it back to a full boil. Process the jars in gently boiling water for 20 minutes. (At altitudes higher than 1,000 feet, longer processing times will be needed.)

4. Remove the jars from the water with a jar lifter, and place them on a rack to cool for 24 hours. As the chutneys cool, a vacuum will form inside the jar, sealing it. A slight indentation in the lid indicates the vacuum seal. Store in a cool, dry, dark place for up to 1 year.

SPICED NUTS

MAKES 2½ CUPS

When the egg white has been properly beaten, no clear liquid will remain on the bottom of the bowl.

- 1 large egg white
- ¼ cup sugar
- 1 teaspoon salt
- ½ teaspoon chile powder
- ¼ teaspoon ground allspice
- ½ teaspoon ground cumin
- 1¾ teaspoons cayenne pepper
- 2½ cups pecan halves or assorted nuts, such as cashews, walnuts, or almonds

1. Heat oven to 300°. Beat egg white until soft and foamy. Combine all remaining ingredients except pecans; whisk into egg white. Stir in pecans until well coated; spread mixture in a single layer onto an ungreased rimmed baking sheet.

2. Bake pecans for 15 minutes, then remove from oven. Using a metal spatula, toss, stir, and separate nuts. Reduce oven to 250°, and return nuts to bake until medium brown, about 10 minutes. Remove from oven; toss, and stir again. Place baking sheet on wire rack to cool (they will crisp up as they cool). Break up any that stick together; store in an airtight container, at room temperature, up to 2 weeks.

CRIMSON AND GOLD
It will keep for months in the refrigerator, but cranberry chutney will likely be consumed long before then. Spread it on Simple White Crackers (page 100) or turkey sandwiches (top). Untie the knotted fabric wrapping made from organza and vintage gold ribbon, and spiced nuts mounded in a bowl are ready to serve (above). Look for special bowls and napkins at tag sales and flea markets.

STRAW TECHNIQUE

Make cheese and poppy-seed straws from one sheet of store-bought puff pastry. Cut the sheet lengthwise, and spread the cheese mixture on one half and the poppy-seed mixture on the other. Cut the dough into strips, twist, and set on a parchment-lined baking sheet. Press each end of the straws with your thumbs to prevent them from untwisting.

CHEESE AND POPPY-SEED STRAWS

MAKES 40

To keep the "twist" in the cheese straws, it is essential that they be very cold when they go into a very hot oven. The standard size for one sheet of frozen puff pastry from a grocery-store box is 10 by 10 inches. If your puff pastry is not this size, cut the width to measure 10 inches. If the length is longer than 10 inches, you will get more straws per sheet and might need more cheese and poppy-seed mixture.

- 1   10-by-10-inch sheet frozen puff pastry (one sheet from a 17.3-ounce package)
- 1   to 2 ounces Parmesan cheese, grated on the small holes of a box grater to yield about $\frac{1}{3}$ cup
- 1   teaspoon cayenne pepper
- 3   tablespoons sesame seeds, lightly toasted
- 3   tablespoons poppy seeds
- $1\frac{1}{2}$ teaspoons coarse salt
- 1   large egg, lightly beaten

1. Thaw puff pastry according to package instructions, just until it is soft enough to cut. (This should take about 20 to 30 minutes at room temperature). Puff pastry should still be very cold. Heat oven to 425° with two racks.

2. In a small bowl, place the cheese and cayenne pepper, and mix to combine. In a second small bowl, combine sesame and poppy seeds with the salt, and set aside.

3. Arrange cold puff pastry on work surface. Cut the puff pastry lengthwise into two equal 5-inch-wide halves. Brush each half with the beaten egg. Sprinkle one half with the cheese mixture and other half with seed mixture. Using a pastry cutter or knife, cut each half crosswise into twenty $\frac{1}{2}$-inch strips.

4. Working one at a time, twist each strip into a double spiral, and transfer to parchment-lined baking sheets, $\frac{1}{2}$ inch apart. Using your thumb, press the ends of the strips down into the parchment to prevent unraveling. Transfer to freezer and chill until very firm, about 20 minutes. (Refrigerator may be used for chilling but will take at least twice as long.) Check dough while chilling to make sure it stays twisted.

5. Transfer the straws to the oven, and bake until golden, rotating baking sheets halfway through cooking time for even browning, 10 to 15 minutes. Cool the straws on a cooling rack. Straws may be made 1 day ahead and kept, in an airtight container, at room temperature.

HERBED GOAT-CHEESE SPREAD

MAKES 2 CUPS

Serve this tangy spread with any of the homemade crackers in this chapter.

- 1   eight-ounce package cream cheese, room temperature
- 1   eleven-ounce package goat cheese, room temperature
- $\frac{3}{4}$ teaspoon salt
- $\frac{1}{4}$ teaspoon freshly ground pepper
- 4   teaspoons freshly squeezed lemon juice
- 3   tablespoons chopped flat-leaf parsley
- 1   tablespoon chopped fresh tarragon
- 1   tablespoon chopped fresh dill
- 1   tablespoon snipped fresh chives

In the bowl of a food processor, process the cream cheese and goat cheese together until creamy and well combined. Add the salt, pepper, lemon juice, parsley, tarragon, dill, and chives; pulse until thoroughly combined, scraping down the sides of the bowl as needed. Transfer spread to an airtight container. Spread will keep, refrigerated, up to 2 days.

OVEN-BAKED SWEET-POTATO CHIPS

MAKES ABOUT 3 DOZEN

These chips are made without any fat. For attractive, circular chips, look for sweet potatoes that are round rather than long. It is best to make very thin slices with a mandoline (see the Guide).

- 1   large sweet potato (about 9 ounces), peel on, washed, and dried
-   Salt and freshly ground pepper

1. Heat oven to 200° with two racks. Line two rimmed baking sheets with parchment paper, and set aside. Using a mandoline, slice the potato crosswise, as thin as possible. Arrange the slices on the prepared sheets, touching as little as possible. Sprinkle lightly with salt and pepper.

2. Cook for 50 minutes. Slices will be dehydrating and shrinking; turn chips over, and rotate baking sheets if needed for even cooking. Cook until slices are crisped and fluted around the edges and the centers are still orange, not brown, 30 to 40 more minutes. Transfer to cooling racks, and cool chips on baking sheets. (Chips will be soft when removed from oven and will crisp as they cool.) Store in an airtight container, at room temperature, up to 3 days.

PHYLLO KNOTS WITH GOAT CHEESE AND SPINACH

MAKES 5½ DOZEN

Once formed, phyllo knots may be frozen, in an airtight container, for one week.

- 6 large scallions, white and green parts, finely chopped
- ⅓ cup olive oil
- 2 ten-ounce packages frozen chopped spinach, thawed, liquid reserved, or 3 pounds fresh spinach, washed and stems removed
- 1 bunch flat-leaf parsley, leaves roughly chopped (about 1 cup)
- 1 bunch dill, roughly chopped (about 1 cup)
- 12 ounces goat cheese, crumbled, room temperature
- 2 large eggs, lightly beaten
  Salt and freshly ground pepper
- 2 one-pound boxes phyllo dough (17-by-11½-inch sheets)
- 2 cups (4 sticks) unsalted butter, melted and kept warm

1. Cook the scallions in the oil, in a large skillet over medium heat, until soft. Add spinach and reserved liquid; cook until warm. Transfer mixture to a thin kitchen towel or cheesecloth; wring liquid into a bowl. Reserve 2 tablespoons liquid, discard the rest. Cool spinach to room temperature.

2. Process spinach, reserved spinach liquid, parsley, dill, goat cheese, eggs, and salt and pepper to taste in a food processor until combined.

3. Heat oven to 425° with two racks. Fill a pastry bag fitted with a #2 tip (or a ⅜-inch-diameter coupler) with spinach mixture. Set aside. Place phyllo flat between two damp kitchen towels. Lay another damp kitchen towel on work surface. Place one phyllo sheet on towel (re-cover remaining phyllo to prevent drying). Brush with butter. Place a second sheet on top; brush with butter. Cut phyllo in half lengthwise and then crosswise to make four pieces. Pipe a line of filling across top of each piece, leaving 1¼ inches on each end. Roll each piece into a tube starting with top-filling side and rolling down toward you, brushing phyllo with butter. Brush completed tube with butter; gently tie into a loose knot.

4. Place on parchment-lined baking sheets. Brush tops with butter. Bake until golden, 15 to 20 minutes, rotating pans halfway through baking. Transfer to cooling racks. Serve warm or at room temperature.

CITRUS AND ROSEMARY OLIVES

MAKES 2 CUPS

- Zest of 1 lemon
- Zest of 1 orange
- 8 to 10 ounces (2 cups) assorted olives, such as niçoise, Nyon, Picholine, kalamata, or Bella di Cerignola
- 2 cloves garlic, minced
- 1 small shallot, minced
- ¼ cup extra-virgin olive oil
- 2 teaspoons minced fresh rosemary or 1 teaspoon crumbled dried rosemary

In a medium bowl, combine the lemon and orange zests with the olives, garlic, shallot, olive oil, and rosemary. Let olives marinate for 2 to 4 hours at room temperature, stirring occasionally. Olive mixture may be kept in an airtight container, in the refrigerator, up to 1 week. Let olives sit at room temperature for at least 30 minutes before serving.

BUTTERMILK-CUMIN CRACKERS

MAKES 60

- 1¼ cups whole-wheat flour, plus more for dusting
- ½ cup toasted wheat germ
- ¼ cup sunflower seeds
- 1 teaspoon ground cumin seeds
- ½ teaspoon baking powder
- ½ teaspoon baking soda
- ½ teaspoon table salt
- 3 tablespoons unsalted butter, cut in pieces
- ½ cup nonfat buttermilk
  Coarse salt for sprinkling
  Vegetable-oil cooking spray

1. Heat oven to 350°. Spray two baking sheets with cooking spray; set aside. In food processor, pulse flour, wheat germ, sunflower seeds, cumin, baking powder, baking soda, and table salt. Add butter; process until mixture resembles coarse meal. With machine running, gradually add buttermilk; process until dough comes together and is moist.

2. Transfer to a lightly floured surface. Allow to rest for 5 minutes. Roll until ¼- to ⅛-inch thick. Sprinkle with coarse salt; roll to press salt into dough.

3. Cut dough into 4-inch-long leaf shapes, or other desired shape. Transfer the leaves to ungreased baking sheets. Pierce each cracker liberally with a fork. Bake until hard, about 16 minutes. Transfer crackers to a wire rack to cool. Store in an airtight plastic container, at room temperature, up to 1 week.

KNOT TECHNIQUES

To shape the phyllo knots, work on a damp kitchen towel to keep the sheets of phyllo moist. Cut the phyllo sheets into four equal pieces. Brush with butter, and pipe a strip of spinach filling along the top of the square (top). Roll the phyllo from the top of the square down toward you, brushing it with butter as you roll. Loosely tie the tubes in knots, just barely tucking one end through the hole (above). Place them on a parchment-lined baking sheet, and bake.

BUTTERMILK-CUMIN CRACKERS *A recipe box lined with gold brocade and pink Japanese papers is the perfect container and serving tray for two cracker shapes: leaves cut freehand, and flowers made from a cutter. Recipe, page 97.*

GIFTS FOR THE HOLIDAY HOST *(opposite, clockwise from top left) Slipknot a length of Bordeaux-colored ribbon around a bottle of Cabernet and attach a cellophane sleeve of walnut blue-cheese coins to it with the free ends of the ribbon. Pair caraway-onion cards and simple white crackers with assertively flavored cheeses such as Mimolette and farmhouse cheddar for an elegant gift. A bamboo steamer is the ideal size to transport chicken-and-mushroom pie to your host's door and can hold two pies at once. Four different cheeses, wrapped in butcher's paper, tied with red waxed twine, and bound with a red satin ribbon, make quick work of holiday gift giving. Choose firm cheeses for easy transport.*

WALNUT BLUE-CHEESE COINS

MAKES 30

These crackers are very rich, yet light and crisp.

- 1 cup toasted walnuts (3¼ ounces)
- ¾ cup all-purpose flour, plus more for dusting
- ½ teaspoon table salt
- ¼ teaspoon freshly ground pepper
- ¼ teaspoon baking soda
- 2 tablespoons cold unsalted butter, cut in pieces
- ¼ pound blue cheese, crumbled

  Coarse salt for sprinkling

1. In a food processor, finely grind ½ cup walnuts. Add the flour, table salt, pepper, and baking soda; pulse to combine. Add butter; pulse until mixture resembles coarse meal. Add cheese; pulse until the dough comes together, about 15 seconds.

2. Heat oven to 350°. Transfer dough to lightly floured surface; divide into two equal parts. Using your hands, roll dough into two 1½-inch-diameter logs. Coarsely chop remaining ½ cup walnuts; sprinkle over a clean work surface. Roll logs in walnuts. Wrap each log in plastic wrap, and chill until firm, at least 3 hours.

3. Slice logs into ¼-inch-thick coins. Transfer to ungreased baking sheet; sprinkle lightly with coarse salt. Bake until centers are firm to touch, about 15 minutes. Transfer to a wire rack to cool. Store in an airtight container, at room temperature, 3 to 4 days.

CARAWAY-ONION CARDS

MAKES ABOUT 2½ DOZEN

- ¼ cup caraway seeds
- 1 cup all-purpose flour, plus more for dusting
- 1 cup rye flour
- ½ teaspoon table salt
- ¼ teaspoon freshly ground pepper
- ½ teaspoon sugar
- 6 tablespoons cold unsalted butter, cut in pieces
- 1 cup minced onion (1 medium onion)
- 1 large egg white

  Coarse salt for sprinkling

1. Heat oven to 350°. Place the caraway seeds in a medium skillet over medium heat. Shaking skillet slightly to keep seeds moving so they do not burn, heat until seeds are aromatic and slightly brown, about 3 minutes. Transfer seeds to a small bowl; set aside.

2. In food processor, pulse the flours, table salt, pepper, sugar, and 2 tablespoons caraway seeds to combine. Add butter; pulse until mixture resembles coarse meal. Add onion; pulse until well combined, about 30 seconds. With machine running, gradually add between 1 and 2 tablespoons cold water, until dough comes together and is stiff. Cover the dough with plastic wrap, and allow to relax at room temperature for 15 to 20 minutes.

3. Transfer dough to a lightly floured surface; roll out to a 14-by-16-inch rectangle, ¹⁄₁₆-inch thick. Cut into about thirty 2-by-3½-inch rectangles.

4. Brush egg white over dough, and sprinkle with remaining 2 tablespoons caraway seeds and coarse salt. Pierce crackers liberally with a fork. Transfer to an ungreased baking sheet, and bake for 20 to 25 minutes, until crackers are lightly browned and firm to the touch, rotating baking sheet if needed for even cooking. Let cool on wire rack. Crackers may be kept in an airtight container, at room temperature, about 1 week.

SIMPLE WHITE CRACKERS

MAKES ABOUT 4 DOZEN

You'll have to discard any scraps, since this dough can't be rolled again.

- 2 cups all-purpose flour, plus more for dusting
- 1 teaspoon table salt
- 2 teaspoons sugar
- 2 tablespoons cold unsalted butter, cut in pieces
- ¾ cup milk

  Coarse salt for sprinkling

1. Heat oven to 325°. In a food processor, pulse flour, table salt, and sugar until combined. Add butter pieces, and pulse until mixture resembles coarse meal. With the machine running, gradually add milk; process until dough comes together. Cover the dough with plastic wrap, and allow to relax at room temperature for 15 to 20 minutes.

2. Unwrap the dough, and transfer it to a lightly floured surface. Roll into 17½-by-17½-inch square, ¹⁄₁₆-inch thick (if the dough continues to spring back, allow to relax again, covered with plastic wrap, for another 10 minutes). Sprinkle dough lightly with coarse salt. Gently press the salt into the dough with the rolling pin.

BREAD TECHNIQUE
The final rise of prosciutto-bread dough takes place right in the eight-pointed pandoro mold (above, see the Guide). Brush the mold liberally with melted butter, gather the ball of dough into its center, and transfer it directly into the mold, seam-side up.

3. Using a knife or pizza cutter, cut dough into 2½-inch squares. With a thin spatula, transfer to ungreased baking sheets. Liberally pierce with fork. Bake for 20 to 25 minutes, until lightly browned and crisp, rotating baking sheets if needed for even cooking. Let cool on wire rack. Keep crackers in an airtight container, at room temperature, about 1 week.

PROSCIUTTO BREAD

MAKES 1 LOAF

Many butchers sell the small ends from their large joints of prosciutto. The ends are perfect to use when making this bread, although unsliced prosciutto can be used. Cover the top of the bread with plastic wrap and parchment before gift wrapping to avoid any grease spotting. Pandoro molds (see the Guide) are traditionally used in Italy for a sweet bread, but any heavy metal 9-cup mold may be used. Cooking times may vary.

- 1 *tablespoon active-dry yeast*
- 2 *teaspoons sugar*
- 4 *cups all-purpose flour*
- 2 *teaspoons coarse salt*
- 2 *teaspoons very coarsely ground pepper*
- ¾ *cup prosciutto, chopped into ¼-inch dice (about 4 ounces)*
- ¾ *cup Italian Fontina cheese, chopped into ¼-inch dice (about 4 ounces)*
   Olive oil for greasing
- 1 *large egg, lightly beaten, for glaze*

1. In bowl of electric mixer fitted with a dough hook, mix yeast and sugar with 1¾ cups warm water (110°), stir until dissolved. Let stand until foamy, 15 minutes.

2. Add flour, salt, and pepper to yeast mixture. Mix on low speed until a smooth ball is formed (dough will be slightly sticky), 5 minutes. Transfer to a lightly floured surface, and pat into a 10-by-10-inch square. Scatter prosciutto and Fontina on top; press in. Pull four corners of dough into center, form a ball, and transfer seam-side down to a lightly oiled large bowl. Cover with plastic wrap. Let rise in warm, draft-free place until doubled in volume, 1 hour.

3. Punch down dough, form into a ball, and turn seam-side down. Cover with plastic wrap, and let rest until doubled in volume, about 1 hour.

4. Heat oven to 425° with rack placed in lower third. Punch down dough, pull four corners of dough into center to form a ball, and place in lightly oiled pandoro mold, seam-side up. Cover with plastic; let rise until it is even with the top of the mold and slightly mounded, 30 minutes. Brush top with egg glaze. Bake until top is a dark golden brown, 35 minutes. Cover bread with a tent of aluminum foil; reduce heat to 350°. Continue baking until base of bread sounds hollow when tapped and sides are golden brown, 30 to 40 minutes. Unmold bread onto cooling rack, top-side down, until completely cool, 1 hour. (If sides of bread are not brown, set bread on oven rack, top-side down, for another 5 minutes, until golden.) Bread will keep wrapped in plastic wrap for 1 to 2 days, although fresh bread always tastes best.

SAVORY BREAD *Parchment-wrapped prosciutto bread (below) packaged in its pretty tin needs little more than two widths of silver metallic ribbon pulled taut over the top of the bread and along the tips and notches of the pandoro mold, and taped on the bottom. A threaded silver bead is on top.*

DOUBLE-CRUST CHICKEN-AND-MUSHROOM PIE

SERVES 6

SESAME GARLAND

*Crisp, golden sesame rounds
can be baked with a hole—
made with a piping tip—
and strung for gift giving. A
square of balsa wood (available
at crafts stores) anchors
each end; a length of seam
binding runs through the
center of each cracker. Slip
the garland into a cellophane
bag for easy transport.*

- 2½ cups plus 6 tablespoons all-purpose flour
- Salt and freshly ground pepper
- 1 teaspoon granulated sugar
- 1 cup (2 sticks) plus 5 tablespoons unsalted butter, cut in small pieces
- 1 three- to four-pound chicken
- 4 cups homemade or low-sodium canned chicken stock
- 8 ounces pearl onions
- 10 ounces red potatoes, scrubbed and cut into ½-inch pieces
- 5 medium carrots, peeled, cut into ½-inch pieces
- 14 ounces shiitake, cremini, or button mushrooms, quartered if large
- ¾ cup milk
- 1 ten-ounce package frozen peas, thawed
- 2 tablespoons fresh thyme leaves
- 2 tablespoons chopped fresh sage
- 1 large egg, beaten with 1 teaspoon water, for glaze

1. Combine 2½ cups flour, 1 teaspoon salt, and the sugar in a food processor. Add 1 cup butter; process until mixture resembles coarse meal, 8 to 10 seconds. Add ¼ to ½ cup ice water in a slow steady stream through feed tube with machine running, until dough holds together, about 30 seconds. Turn dough onto piece of plastic wrap; divide in half. Press each half into flat circles, wrap each in plastic, and refrigerate at least 1 hour or overnight.

2. Place chicken and stock in a medium stockpot. Add enough water just to cover chicken. Bring to a boil, reduce heat, simmer gently until chicken is cooked through, 45 minutes. Using tongs, transfer chicken to a plate; set aside until cool enough to handle. Strain 2 cups stock into a measuring cup; and set aside. (Remaining stock may be frozen for another use.)

3. Heat oven to 375° with rack in center. Cook pearl onions in a medium pan of simmering water, 15 minutes. Drain; rinse under cool water. Peel onions; set aside. Remove skin and bones from chicken; discard. Shred chicken into bite-size pieces; set aside.

4. Melt remaining butter in a large high-sided skillet over medium heat. Add potatoes, carrots, and onions, and cook, stirring occasionally, until potatoes begin to turn golden. Add mushrooms; cook 5 minutes more. Add remaining flour, and cook,

stirring for 1 minute. Add reserved chicken stock and milk; bring to a simmer. Cook until thick and bubbly, stirring constantly. Stir in reserved chicken, peas, thyme, sage, and salt and pepper to taste. Remove from heat, and let cool slightly.

5. On a lightly floured surface, roll out half the dough to a 12-inch circle. Transfer dough to a 9½-inch glass pie plate with dough overlapping top of pan. Trim dough to about a 1-inch overhang. Carefully spoon filling into dough.

6. Roll out remaining dough to a 10-inch circle, transfer to top of filling. Fold overlapping edges of dough under to make a firm edge. Use fingers to pinch a decorative border. Use a knife to make four to five slits into the center of the pie. Brush top of dough with egg glaze. Bake pie on a baking sheet until dough is golden brown, rotating pie halfway through for even baking, 45 to 60 minutes.

SESAME ROUNDS

MAKES 26

- 1 cup all-purpose flour, plus more for dusting
- ½ teaspoon table salt
- ⅛ teaspoon freshly ground black pepper
- 1 teaspoon freshly grated lemon zest
- Pinch cayenne
- 2 tablespoons chopped fresh thyme
- 3 tablespoons sesame seeds, unhulled
- 2 tablespoons unsalted butter, cut in pieces
- 1 large egg white
- Coarse salt for sprinkling

1. Heat oven to 350°. In a food processor, pulse flour, table salt, black pepper, lemon zest, cayenne, thyme, and 2 tablespoons sesame seeds. Add butter; pulse until mixture resembles coarse meal. With machine running, add ¼ cup cold water; process until the dough comes together.

2. Transfer the dough to lightly floured surface, and divide it into two equal parts. Roll out to ⅛-inch thickness. Cut into 2½-inch circles, and transfer to an ungreased baking sheet.

3. Brush egg white over rounds; sprinkle with remaining tablespoon sesame seeds and coarse salt. Bake 20 to 25 minutes, until firm to the touch. Let cool on wire rack. Store in an airtight plastic container, at room temperature, up to 1 week.

part 3

GREETINGS
AND
WRAPPINGS

REMEMBER WHEN HEAVEN MEANT SCISSORS, COLORED PAPER, SCRAPS OF PRETTY FABRIC, BELLS, BUTTONS, A JAR OF THICK WHITE PASTE— AND NO ONE TO BOTHER YOU? ADD A PILE OF PRESENTS, AND YOU CAN RETURN TO THAT TIME AGAIN THIS HOLIDAY SEASON. FORGET THE BUSTLE AND THE BUYING, THE SHOPPING AND SELECTING. ADORN YOUR GIFTS WITH CARDS, WRAPS, AND TAGS THAT YOU'VE MADE YOURSELF.

Transform
plain paper
into cheerful
greetings with
a few snips
and stitches,
buttons
and bows

HANDMADE
CARDS

Melanie

Lace a ribbon through a folded piece of colored paper, tie it with a festive bow, and a simple greeting card becomes a special gift—a treat to open and a pleasure to display. Handmade cards take just moments to craft, yet they convey the holiday spirit better than any you can buy.

With notions from your sewing box, a few art supplies, and some flights of fancy, it's easy to create original and personal cards that are sure to delight everyone on your mailing list. Who can resist the whimsical smile beaming from your button snowman? ✳ Materials for homemade cards can be as varied as your imagination, although paper is the fundamental medium. Use different weights, textures, colors, and patterns to give a unique feel to each project. Ribbons are essential, too, as a wrapping, fastener, or hanger. And swatches of felt and other fabrics, twine, or small pom-poms can provide distinctive decorations. ✳ Templates for some card elements are in this book, or you may draft models of your own. And while traditional motifs are always appropriate, don't neglect modern tools for making cards—color photocopiers and computer printers make quick work of multiple photo cards and cocktail cards. ✳ Handmade cards deserve special packaging too: Slip them into glassine envelopes to both display and protect them. Send fragile and three-dimensional cards in padded mailers, or leave them on an office mate's desk or a neighbor's doorstep.

BUTTON SNOWMEN *Tiny knots in red, white, and black embroidery thread bring these shirt-button snowmen (opposite) to life. To hide the stitches securing the buttons, each card is made of two pieces of paper; color-coordinated ribbon secures all the pieces together and can be used to hang the cards from the tree. Because buttons are fragile, the cards should be mailed in padded envelopes. For more instructions, see page 110.*

RIBBON TREES *Taking needle and thread to paper is a tidier alternative to tape and glue. Scraps of ribbon in graduating lengths are arranged to form a tree, the sewn "trunk" securing them to the paper. Using pinking shears, cut the ribbon ends at right angles to create a feathery look to the tree branches (above left) or on slanted angles for a more symmetrical tree (above right). For more instructions, see page 110.*

GIFT-WRAPPED CARDS *Dressing a card as a present can be as easy as tying a bow. These ribbon-tied cards can be decorated as simply or elaborately as you wish with anything you would use to adorn a package. We added a gift tag to a card tied with pink seam binding (above left) and used a rubber stamp to print the year on a piece of ½-inch-thick rose satin ribbon (center right). The large letters that spell "noel" (center left) are written with a pen and opaque white ink. For how-to instructions, see page 110. Any of the cards in this chapter would make an elegant ornament for the greetings tree found on page 29. Just punch a hole in the top of the card and tie it to a beaded ribbon. Or make a garland of gift-wrapped cards in graduated sizes like the one on page 30 to hang from the mantel.*

ACCORDION TREES

A card that closes with a bow hints at a surprise, and these, tied with grosgrain ribbons, don't disappoint. Each time the card opens, a tree made from pleated paper rectangles pops up, like a small gift. Although the trees can be glued into any size card, they are especially attractive in tall, slender cards (right). For more how-to instructions, see page 110.

CREATING CARDS WITH RIBBONS AND PAPER

button snowmen, gift-wrapped cards, accordion trees, and ribbon trees

BUTTON SNOWMEN To make these (left), you'll need card stock in two weights, medium and heavy; white buttons in graduating sizes; clear-drying craft glue; needle and colored thread (we used red, white, and black); a hole punch; and ribbon. Fold medium-weight card stock in half to form a card; fold heavier card stock over it. Glue three buttons onto heavier stock to represent a snowman. Position top-button holes to form a face when filled in with knots of colored thread. (If buttons have four holes, line up top button's holes to form a square; holes of two lower buttons should form a diamond.) Poke a hole through just the top card and each buttonhole. To make eyes, thread needle with black thread, knot at end, and pull through top buttonhole from behind top card. Make another knot close to the button; poke needle back through same button hole to back of card. Bring needle back through second eyehole; repeat process for it and for additional buttonholes. For mouth, sew across two holes on top button with red thread. To secure cards together, punch two holes through top of each, thread ribbon through holes, and tie in a bow.

GIFT-WRAPPED CARDS Fold a piece of card stock in half or use a store-bought card. You'll also need a utility knife and ribbon (below left). To tie a bow onto a card, use the utility knife to make a vertical slit the width of the ribbon in the middle of the card's spine (make the slit higher or lower if you want the bow to be off center). Thread the ribbon through the slit, wrap it around the front panel of the card as if wrapping a gift, and tie a bow in front. If you wish, slip a gift tag onto the ribbon before you tie it.

ACCORDION TREES Fold a piece of card stock in half or use a store-bought card. You'll also need scissors or a utility knife, colored kraft paper, a ruler, a bone folder (available at art-supply stores), craft glue, a hole punch, and ribbon (below center). Cut kraft paper into rectangles of graduating lengths and widths. Pleat each rectangle accordion-style; score folds with bone folder. Open card, and center rectangles in spine of card. Glue down ends to form a pop-up tree, which will expand as you open card. To make the "bucket" that holds the tree, fold another paper rectangle into four accordion folds. Glue two ends on either side of card's spine. If you wish, use a star-shaped hole punch (see the Guide) to make a star for top of tree. Punch holes on outer edges of card, thread ribbon through each hole, and knot ends to hold in place. Close the card, and tie the ribbons in a bow.

RIBBON TREES To make these cards, you'll need ⅜-inch-thick grosgrain ribbon (we used two colors), pinking shears, blank store-bought cards or card stock, low-tack or drafting tape (see the Guide), and a sewing machine. Cut ribbon with shears into lengths that diminish in size to form a tree shape. Center strips on front of card, trim ends (straight or on an angle), and secure them with two pieces of tape. Run center of "tree" through sewing machine vertically (below right) to create a thread "trunk." Knot each end on the back side of the card, trim, and remove tape.

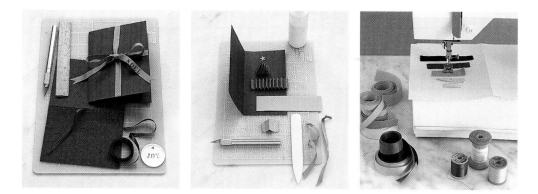

CRAFTING CARDS WITH FAMILY PHOTOS

a mini photo album and a favorite picture for framing

PHOTO CARDS When making this ribbon-trimmed accordion-fold card (above left), use color copies of photographs rather than originals because photocopies are thinner and can be reduced to fit. You'll also need medium to heavyweight art paper, craft glue, scissors, and round white stickers. Fold the paper into four sections. Write a greeting on the first of the four quarters, and glue photographs on the remaining three. For the trim, cut two pieces of ribbon, about 10 inches long. Then cut a vertical slit (slightly wider than the ribbon) into the center of one edge of the card. String ribbon through slit from behind; secure and cover the end with a sticker. Repeat on other end of card. Fold the card, wrap the ribbons around it, and tie them in a bow. Photos can also be placed on blank cards (above right) with glue or self-adhesive photo corners. For these, you'll need blank cards, glue or photo corners, glassine envelopes, and labels. If using corners, place the photograph on card, and outline its corners with a pencil. Remove adhesive backing from photo corners, place over pencil marks, and insert a photo. Write a message on the card underneath the picture, and slip it into a glassine envelope; or put the card in the envelope first, stick a label on the envelope, and write a greeting or address on it. Either way, the translucent envelope becomes part of the card, and the photo can be removed and placed in a frame or album after the holidays.

MAKING HOLIDAY SILHOUETTES

snowflakes, paper stockings, ornament cards, and cocktail cards

SNOWFLAKES With Fiskars scissors (left, see the Guide) and origami paper, snowflake cards (opposite, top left) are much easier to make than they look: The scissors are extra sharp and have a micropoint to ensure crisp, intricate work; origami paper is thin and square, which makes folding and cutting quick, not cumbersome. For this project, you will also need glassine envelopes (to contain the snowflakes, which are delicate—and tear easily—when presented on their own), a hole punch, and lengths of string. To make a snowflake, fold a piece of origami into even quarters, and draw a pattern on it, copying from a model or tracing our template on page 135. Cut out the shape, and unfold the paper. Place the resulting snowflake in a glassine envelope either alone or against a colored-paper backdrop. A greeting can be written on the paper. Punch a hole in one or two corners of the envelope, and attach a loop of string so the card can be displayed by hanging it on a Christmas tree, a doorknob, or a window.

PAPER STOCKINGS To create multiples of this appealing card (opposite, top right), make a template by drawing a stocking shape on a piece of cardboard or use our template on page 133; the one we made is approximately 5 inches long. Make another template for a cuff for the stocking. You'll also need stiff patterned and colored papers (available at art-supply stores), pinking shears, needle and thread, pom-poms, a hole punch, ribbon, and glassine envelopes. With a pencil, trace the stocking onto a piece of paper. Place a second sheet of paper under the first, and sew the two pieces together, stitching along the lines. Cut out the sewn stocking with the pinking shears, allowing for a ¼-inch border outside the stitches. Trace the cuff template onto different-colored paper, and cut out. Stitch small pom-poms to the edge of the cuff (if you plan to mail your cards in a regular envelope, decorate instead with velvet ribbon, metallic braid, or rickrack). Glue the cuff to the front of the stocking. Punch a hole in upper corner, slip narrow ribbon through, and tuck a greeting inside stocking. Place in a glassine envelope alone or against a piece of colored paper.

ORNAMENT CARDS These cheerful cards are easy to make and can be as bold and colorful as you like (opposite, bottom left). You'll need stiff patterned paper (available at art-supply stores), scissors, store-bought cards or card stock folded into cards, a hole punch, waxed twine, and glassine envelopes. Draw a template, or use ours on page 134, for an ornament on a piece of cardboard; cut it out; and place it on the patterned paper. Trace around the template with a pencil, then cut out ornament. Punch holes at the top of the ornament and the card. Secure together with waxed twine. Write your message inside the card, and place in a glassine envelope.

COCKTAIL CARDS Some people prefer to send holiday cards to toast the New Year. These paper cocktail cards (opposite, bottom right), imprinted with recipes for cocktails and tucked into a translucent envelope, may come in handy at a party or two. You'll need: a ruler, heavy paper, construction or laser-printer paper, scissors, and glassine envelopes. Measure the envelopes you plan to use. Trace our template on page 135 onto a heavy piece of paper. (Glasses should be large enough in length or width to almost fill envelopes.) Trace template onto construction or laser-printer paper. To inscribe the cocktail recipes and holiday wishes, print them out on a computer or write them by hand, adjusting the lines of text to fit into the shape of the glass. You can also take the recipe and greeting to a rubber-stamp maker. With a stamp, dozens of cards can be created in minutes. Cut out glasses with recipes printed on them, and place them in glassine envelopes alone or against a backdrop of patterned paper.

A few colors,
folds, and
flourishes
turn any
present into a
work of art

WRAPS,
TAGS,
BUNDLES,
AND
BOWS

There are moments in the holiday weeks so exquisite, we wish they could last forever. The clear light of a winter morning illuminates the tinseled branches of a tree. Underneath is an array of boxes cloaked in shimmering layers of paper, trimmed with soft bows and crisp ruffles

of paper. ✷ And suddenly the mood changes. The time for gift giving arrives, and all the care and craft of our brilliantly wrapped gifts disappear in an instant, as bows are untied, ribbons unwound, and paper peeled off and cast aside. ✷ Gift wrap—like a decorated cake—is ephemeral. But while an elaborate dessert brings us fleeting pleasure, at least we can enjoy

a display of gorgeous gifts for the duration of the holiday season. Not, of course, if you only leave a few rushed minutes for gift wrapping late on Christmas Eve. With planning and organization (and a few hours of delightful concentration) you can turn every gift into a tempting work of art. ✷ Think of presents as a collection rather than as an assortment of individual pieces. Pick a palette, then

GIFT TREE *No need to wait for Santa—wrap your presents as soon as you can, and arrange them together in a prominent place. A silver feather tree sparkling with vintage ornaments and topped with a red satin bow (opposite) echoes the colors of the glistening papers and ribbons on gifts (above) tucked underneath. For instructions on how to make the paper loop-the-loop bow from scraps of paper, see page 121.*

vary the materials. Or wrap all your packages in the same paper and then bind them in ribbons of different colors. Or swath them in different papers, and tie them all with the same ribbon. The color scheme does not have to be limited to classic red and green— choose papers in shades of gold and accent them with ribbons ranging from deep maroon to bright red—but it should complement the colors and textures of the wreaths, garlands, and other ornaments nearby. ✳ You won't need a lot of expensive materials to make the beautiful packages shown on the following pages. Tissue comes in delectable colors and is particularly good for wrapping soft packages; it's more forgiving than heavy paper, and can be ironed smooth on the lowest setting if it crinkles. Kraft paper also makes a lovely wrapping for soft gifts; tie these with twine and dress them up with an evergreen sprig snipped from the tree. ✳ Many materials for wrapping gifts can be collected over the year. Recycle pretty papers and trimmings from the gifts you receive. Save short lengths of seam binding to fashion enchanting bows. Wrap your packages in wallpaper remnants, and embellish them with bands of the same paper rolled into ruffles or floppy bows. Create a bag or box, like the one on page 119, for all these found treasures, and add swatches of paper, snippets of ribbon, and decorative miniatures, like millinery fruit or jingle bells, throughout the year. ✳ For ideas, look closely at every page of this book. In addition to the techniques for gift presentation in this chapter, you will find many more in Cookies and Confections page 64; Gifts for a Long, Long List, page 80; and Savories for Gifts and Gatherings, page 92.

PAPER PINWHEELS
A toy attached to a gift heightens the anticipation of the surprise that's inside. The vanes of these pinwheels (opposite), cut from wrapping paper glued to heavier paper stock, complement the lustrous wrapping and ribbons on the gifts they adorn. Use remnants of satin and grosgrain ribbon and seam binding to create luxurious bands for tucking the pinwheel between. For instructions on how to make a pinwheel, see page 121.

FOUR WRAPPING IDEAS

paper plus ribbon—choose one as your theme, and vary the other

SAME PAPER, DIFFERENT RIBBONS A merry mix of ribbons, twine, and ornaments brings character, whimsy, and individuality to gifts wrapped identically in silver tissue (opposite, top left). To make gift wrapping less hectic, buy a large amount of paper in one color and wrap gifts as you acquire them. Tissue costs less than most wrapping papers and comes in a variety of wonderful hues. Use an adhesive note to identify each gift's recipient as you wrap it, then store until the holidays (this page, bottom right). Ribbons and tags can get crushed, so don't add them until you're ready to unveil your gifts. Decorating packages is much easier if you collect the materials all year in a box (bottom left). Save bits of ribbons, seam binding, and twine along with decorative fruit, silk leaves, and miniature Christmas ornaments for adorning packages. To distinguish identically wrapped presents, vary the color, width, and texture of the ribbons. Even a snippet of beautiful ribbon is effective when knotted over twine.

SAME RIBBON, DIFFERENT PAPER Although the green satin ribbons that adorn these silver-and-white packages were cut from the same bolt, they're tied in different ways (opposite, top right). Using the same type of ribbon is an attractive way to unify packages wrapped in different papers. The papers are a mix of solid colors and simple geometric prints that can be used any time of year; to make them festive, we added green ribbons, gift tags, and the silk leaves slipped under the simple bows.

KRAFT PAPER Presents do not need the crisp lines and sharp corners of a gift box to be appealing. Victorian-style bundles (opposite, bottom left) wrapped in kraft paper and twine hint at the gifts' shapes and invite you to guess what's inside. Embellishments are simple but appealing: evergreen sprigs, bits of ribbon, and red gift tags. Under the kraft-paper covering, each gift is wrapped in bright-red tissue and tied with more twine.

ASSIGNING COLORS Gift tags are nice to put on presents for friends, but they aren't necessary on gifts for family members if each is assigned a different color wrapping (this page, above right). Choose papers in solid hues that will complement one another and enhance the colors on your tree. These packages are tied with paper ribbon.

MAKING GIFT TAGS With stationery-store supplies, ribbon pieces, greenery sprigs, and a hole punch, these gift tags (opposite, bottom right) are inexpensive and fun to make. Clockwise from top left: The kraft-paper leaves have pinked edges; a bunch of millinery berries and a velvet ribbon are threaded through a hole punched in the corner. A round paper tag and holly sprig are affixed with a narrow silver ribbon to a backdrop of two silver-foil seals glued together. A red ribbon and miniature-sled ornament embellish a green stationery tag. Tiny glass balls, a boxwood sprig, and gold organdy ribbon dress a round key tag. A mini pinecone, a balsam sprig, and a gold bell adorn a red stationery tag tied with two-tone ribbon. A crisp plaid ribbon and little silk leaves turn a plain piece of white paper into a charming gift tag.

MAKING PAPER GIFT DECORATIONS
loop-the-loop, ruffle top, floppy bow, and pinwheel

LOOP-THE-LOOP Make "bows" from rolled paper to use up scraps of wrapping. For the "bow" on page 115, you will need a 4"-by-4"-by-3" box; four 10"-by-1¼" strips; four 11"-by-1" strips; four 1½"-by-½" strips. (See how-to opposite.) 1. Trim ends of 10" strips into V shape. Center two strips on top of box; cross over with remaining two strips. 2. Trim one end of each 11" strip into V shape; curl other end into a circle that's about 1½" in diameter. Place one of these strips on left side of one crisscrossed pair already in place. Continue placing others in a pinwheel fashion, circles abutting in middle. Form 1½"-strips into circles; tape inside each larger circle.

RUFFLE TOP Patterned wrapping papers (above right) work nicely for these projects because you can play with their directions. You'll need a 8¼"-by-8"-by-6" box, two 22"-by-3" strips; eight 2"-by-1" strips; twelve 2½"-by-2" strips; two 10½"-by-1" strips; two 8½"-by-1¾" strips; and four 5"-by-2" strips. (See how-to opposite.) 1. Trim ends of 22" strips in scallop shape. Tape center of each strip to box top, 1" in from sides as shown. Tape strips, 3" from scalloped ends, to sides of box, 1½" down from edge; strip should be loose and flowing. Tape ends of four 2" strips together to form circles; place on side of box inside bowed-out portions of scalloped strips. 2. Form 2½", 10½", and 8½" strips into circles (12 small, 2 medium, and 2 large). Tape a row of circles along one bowed strip as shown: 3 small, 1 large, 3 small. Alternate patterns as you go. Tape medium circle inside large one. Repeat along second bowed strip. Form 5" strips into circles; attach to sides just under bottom of scalloped edges to make edges stand out off box. Form remaining 2" strips into circles, and tape them inside bigger circles on the sides.

FLOPPY BOW Papers that are flexible but not too lightweight are best for making decorations from rolled strips (opposite, left). You'll need a 6"-by-4½"-by-4½" box, two 24"-by-1" strips (or, if paper is not long enough, cut two 12"-by-1" strips); two 17"-by-1" strips; two 13½"-by-1" strips; two 10½"-by-1" strips; two 6"-by-1" strips; and two 3"-by-1" strips. (See how-to below.) 1. Tape ends of each strip together to form a circle. Pinch top and bottom of each circle, except the smallest circle, together to form two loops. (If using 12" strips, form each into one loop. Tape together at their ends to form one large piece with two loops.) Tape one of the two largest pieces in center of box top; loops should cascade down sides of box. Place second large piece over first so they crisscross. Repeat with remaining pieces, building bow with longest pieces on bottom and shortest on top. Place last circle in center of bow.

PAPER PINWHEEL Tie a pinwheel around a package instead of a bow (see page 117). To make one, you'll need a thin dowel or skewer (clip off its pointed end), a utility knife, paint, coordinating sheets of origami, wrapping, or other lightweight paper, Spray Mount adhesive, a ruler, a push pin, a map pin, and a bead. Cut dowel or skewer to desired length; paint and let dry. Choose two coordinating sheets of the paper. Cut a square from each the size you'd like your pinwheel to be (our squares range from three to six inches). Use the spray mount to glue squares together. Fold in half, diagonally, and in half again, then unfold. 1. Cut along each crease two-thirds of way to square's center, dividing each corner into two points. 2. Bring every other point to center so points overlap. Hold in place, poke the push pin through center, and, keeping all four points in place, remove push pin. Insert the map pin into hole formed (the push-pin hole is slightly larger than circumference of the map pin, enabling the pinwheel to spin). 3. Thread a small bead onto map pin behind the wheel, and poke pin into the dowel, ½" from top. To prevent wood from splitting, soak the dowel tip in water before inserting the map pin.

LOOP-THE-LOOP

RUFFLE TOP

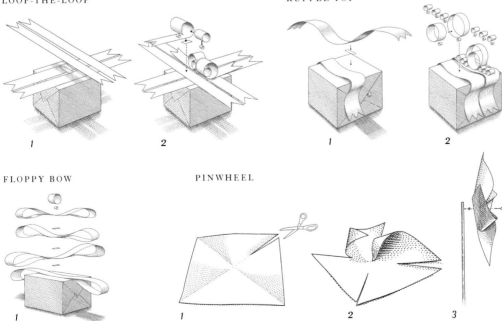

FLOPPY BOW

PINWHEEL

WRAPPING FRAGILE GIFTS

custom "boxes" and grass cushions

PYRAMID PACKAGE Fragile gifts can be encased in a paper pyramid, a design borrowed from French pastry shops (right). This wrapping works best if the gift weighs a quarter-pound or more; the weight helps the paper stay put while you're folding. Place gift on 4½-inch square cardboard pallet (a box lid works well). Center pallet on a 20"-by-11" piece of tissue paper. Below: 1. Bring the short sides of tissue up so they meet at top. Holding in place with your left hand, fold the front side of paper inward, pressing it down along bottom edge of pallet, creasing it as shown. 2. Fold back side of paper inward and down at a 30-degree angle from the point at the top made by your left hand; continue folding three or four times, until the paper comes to a neat point. 3. Turn package, and repeat with other side. Fold points under bottom of package; secure with a sticker. Pass a ¼-inch-wide ribbon under the bottom, bring ends up, and cinch the ribbon around pyramid an inch below the tip. Tie ends of ribbon to make a loop handle.

SOFT PACKAGE Rather than relegating an odd-shaped gift to a box, nestle it in a cloud of Easter grass, and encase it in a pillow-shaped package. Bottom: 1. Center gift in Easter grass in middle of a square of tissue paper large enough so that opposite sides overlap by 1 inch when folded to center. Fold two sides inward and hold in place with one hand; fold other two sides to points, one at a time with your free hand. 2. Fold points to center; secure with tape. 3. Turn the package over, and twist the corners into piglet ears; cinch them with an 8-inch length of ribbon. Soft packages look appealing piled in graduated sizes, and tied with wide ribbon (opposite).

The pleasures
of celebration
and the
joys of giving
meet at the
holiday table

FAVORS
FOR A
HOLIDAY
FEAST

beaded napkin wraps

organza stockings

monogrammed cookies

tiny trees

springerle wreaths

A grand holiday dinner is a gift we share with our friends and family, and a carefully laid table is the elegant wrapping in which it comes. It's not for the sake of formality that we dress our tables with china, crystal, and our best linens with silverware tucked inside. Beautiful settings lend excitement and spirit to the feast—polished surfaces reflect the sparkle of a fire in the hearth and candlelight around the table. And the musical pings and clinks of stemware and china add to the merriment and chatter. ✳ But the settings we show in this chapter incorporate actual gifts, too—at every place, there's a party favor and a personal token, in the guise of a place tag or napkin decoration. A silver ribbon with a crystal-chandelier pendant is used as an elegant napkin band, but when taken home will become a tree ornament; springerle cookies molded in the shape of wreaths can be used the same way. Cookie dough is baked into glittering, edible monograms to guide guests to their seats. Another charming way to present napkins is to wrap them into old-fashioned English Christmas crackers: These will not explode with quite such a bang, but will burst with small presents and toys. Children will enjoy making these lovely favors, as they will two other gift ideas here: a monogrammed beaded napkin wrap strung on waxed twine, and a tiny Christmas-tree place card made from a sprig of greenery and a round of kindling.

MONOGRAMMED COOKIES
Used instead of place cards, these cookies not only direct guests to their seats, they make tantalizing favors to be eaten along with holiday desserts. The cookies are sprinkled with luster dust to complement the antique pink lustreware plates and pale-pink napkins. The dessert plates sit atop antique Minton salt-glaze dinner plates embellished with a raised strawberry-and-leaf border. See page 129 for recipe and how-to.

SETTING A HOLIDAY TABLE WITH FAVORS

organza stocking, Christmas cracker, tiny tree, beaded napkin wrap, and springerle wreath

TABLETOP TOKENS The most unforgettable place cards are the ones guests can take home. Opposite, clockwise from top left: A stocking, made from kraft paper and organza, holds a candy cane. Napkins make handsome Christmas crackers, folded around a corrugated paper roll filled with tiny gifts and candies. Personalize a place setting by tying a napkin with waxed twine strung with beads and a guest's initials. A paper star atop a sprig of greenery set into a kindling-block base makes a fragrant and charming place card.

ORGANZA STOCKING To make this place card (opposite, top left), use the small-stocking template on page 133. Trace template onto a piece of colored kraft paper and a piece of stiff organza, and cut out. Using a paint pen, write guest's name at the top of the paper stocking. Pin the two pieces together, wrong sides facing, at the toe, heel, and instep. Machine stitch around stocking, ½-inch from the edge, leaving the top open. Trim edges with pinking shears. If you like, sew a looped piece of silver cord or ribbon at the top of the seam on the heel side for hanging. Slip a candy cane or other holiday sweet inside.

CHRISTMAS CRACKER A quiet but no less surprising version of traditional Christmas crackers, these table favors (opposite, top right) must be opened before dinner begins; the wrapping paper is the guest's napkin. To make the crackers, cut a piece of corrugated paper to form a tube, and secure with tape. Place candies or small gifts inside. Position tube in the middle of one edge of an unfolded napkin. Roll napkin around tube; there should be excess napkin fabric on either end of tube. Place a length of ribbon lengthwise along the tube. Tie one end around the excess fabric, and knot. Pull ribbon along the length of the tube to the opposite end, tie around the excess fabric, and knot. Cut a circle from a piece of colored kraft paper, and write the guest's name on it. Punch holes on either side of the name, thread a length of silk cord through holes, and tie cord to each end of cracker.

TINY TREE When you're chopping firewood, set aside branches that are too thin for logs and too thick for kindling. Use them instead as the base for this festive holiday place card (opposite, bottom left). Cut a branch (ours is black walnut) into thin rounds. Drill a hole in the center with a high-speed rotary drill or a regular drill with a small bit. Insert sprigs of greenery (we used dwarf Alberta spruce), and position a cut-out paper-ornament name tag in the top of the branch, or tie on with colored twine. And don't forget to place a star on top.

BEADED NAPKIN WRAP To make these favors (opposite, bottom right), fold napkin in a square. Using an extra-long length of twine, wrap napkin as you would a gift box, beginning on top side and crisscrossing the twine on the underside. Tie in a knot on top where the twine intersects. String several beads and your guest's initials on free ends of twine, and knot at the bottom.

SPRINGERLE WREATH To make these elegant serving accents (see page 128), lay napkin out flat. Fold top edge of napkin down to middle of napkin. Turn napkin over. Fold bottom edge of napkin up to middle of napkin. Turn napkin so folded edge is perpendicular to your body, and roll, creating a pocket (left). Thread narrow ribbon through center of springerle (see recipe, page 129), making sure free ends of ribbon are even. Tie ribbon in a knot to hold cookie in place. Wrap ribbon around napkin, and tie in back. Place silverware in pocket.

SPRINGERLE-WREATH NAPKIN WRAPS *What prettier way to present the silver for a buffet than in these napkin "pockets," tied with narrow satin ribbon looped through wreath-shaped springerle cookies? Guests can eat them, or take them home to hang on a tree. See napkin instruction, page 126, and cookie recipe, opposite.*

MONOGRAMMED COOKIES

MAKES 1 DOZEN

- 4 cups sifted all-purpose flour
- ½ teaspoon salt
- ½ teaspoon baking powder
- 1 cup (2 sticks) unsalted butter, room temperature
- 2 cups sugar
- 2 large eggs
- 2 teaspoons pure vanilla extract
- ¼ cup sanding sugar (see the Guide)
  Luster dust (see the Guide)
- 2 large egg whites, lightly beaten

1. In a large bowl, sift together flour, salt, and baking powder; set aside. With an electric mixer, cream butter and sugar on medium speed until fluffy and white, 5 minutes. Add eggs, one at a time, and continue beating until combined. Beat in vanilla.

2. Gradually add flour mixture; mix on low until combined. Transfer dough to work surface; divide into two halves. Flatten each into a rectangle; wrap in plastic wrap. Chill 1 hour.

3. On a lightly floured surface, roll out one piece of dough until thin, no more than ⅛-inch thick. With a 2¾-inch-square-fluted cookie cutter, cut out 12 cookies; transfer with spatula to parchment-lined baking sheet. Repeat with remaining dough for 12 more cookies on a second baking sheet. Cut out the 12 desired letters using alphabet-cookie cutters from remaining dough (chill dough if difficult to cut). Transfer letters to baking sheets. Transfer baking sheets to freezer for 25 minutes or until firm.

4. Transfer baking sheets to work surface. Using a 1 ¾-inch-square-fluted cookie cutter, cut out 12 centers from 12 cold cookies to create the top "frame" section (top right). Discard cut-out center pieces of dough. Do not reroll scraps. Return baking sheets to freezer; chill dough until firm, about 25 minutes.

5. Heat oven to 400° with 2 racks. Remove sheets from freezer; assemble cookies before baking. Align one frame on top of one base, repeat with remaining cookies. Center one letter in middle of each cookie. Rechill dough if warm. Bake until just beginning to color on sides, 8 to 12 minutes, rotating pans halfway through baking. Transfer sheets to cooling racks; cool. Cookies may be made up to this point stored in an airtight container, at room temperature, for 1 day.

6. Transfer sanding sugar to a small bowl. Using a toothpick, transfer tiny amounts of luster dust to sugar. Stir until combined; repeating until desired shade is reached. Brush egg white in center of cookie, working carefully around letter. Sprinkle sugar over egg white. Repeat with remaining cookies. Store in 1 layer in an airtight container, at room temperature, up to 1 day.

SPRINGERLE WREATHS

MAKES 56 WREATHS

- 6 large eggs, at room temperature
- 6 cups sifted confectioners' sugar, plus more for dusting
- 8 tablespoons (1 stick) unsalted butter, at room temperature, cut in pieces
- ½ teaspoon salt
- 1¼ teaspoons anise extract
- 10 to 11 cups sifted cake flour
  Luster dust (see the Guide)

1. With an electric mixer fitted with a whisk attachment, beat eggs on high until thick and lemon colored, 12 minutes. Reduce to medium low; add confectioners' sugar, one cup at a time, beating well after each addition, until creamy, 2 minutes.

2. Increase speed to high, and add butter, 1 tablespoon at a time, beating until creamy, about 1 minute. Add salt and anise extract; beat to combine.

3. Set mixer on medium low, and add 8 cups flour, 1 cup at a time, until a soft dough is formed. Change to a paddle attachment; add 1 more cup flour, mixing until well combined (or mix by hand).

4. Transfer dough to surface sprinkled with 1 cup flour; knead until incorporated, 5 minutes. If dough is still sticky, add up to 1 cup more flour, a little at a time. Divide into 4 pieces; cover with plastic wrap.

5. Dust a work surface with confectioners' sugar; roll out 1 piece of dough to a ⅜-inch thickness. Working quickly, press the mold (see the Guide) firmly into dough. Remove mold. Using a knife, cut out each shape (above right). Using a spatula, transfer to a parchment-lined cooling rack set over a baking sheet, spaced 1 inch apart. Repeat, rolling out remaining dough (dough scraps should be rekneaded and rolled out again), dusting surface with confectioners' sugar as needed. Let springerle stand, uncovered, for 24 hours. Turn over; let stand another 24 hours.

6. Working in batches, arrange springerle, pattern-side up, on ungreased baking sheets. Bake at 200° for 1 to 2 hours, until dry. Cool on a cooling rack. To decorate, use a small brush to lightly brush luster dust onto springerle. Store in an airtight container, at room temperature, for 2 to 3 weeks.

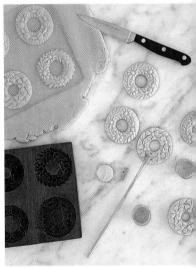

COOKIE TECHNIQUES
Cookie dough must be well chilled before it is rolled very thin on a lightly floured surface (top) to make monogrammed cookies. (For cookie cutters, see the Guide). Press a springerle mold very firmly into the dough to make a sharp impression (above). The wreaths are cut out with a knife and brushed with luster dust.

WINTER-WHITE TABLE *Crystal stemware and crystal chandelier pieces tied around napkins with silver ribbons glisten like dewdrops on a table set in grays and whites. Guests can take the napkin rings home to hang on their Christmas tree by snipping the narrow silver twine off the wider ribbon and tying it into a loop for a hanger. For how-to, see opposite page.*

MAKING CRYSTAL NAPKIN BANDS *Cut metallic silver ribbon and silver metallic twine in equal lengths long enough to tie around a folded napkin. Pin metallic twine to center of ribbon. With a needle and silver thread, hand stitch the twine to the ribbon in three places. Remove the wire loop at the top of the chandelier piece. Find the middle of the ribbon band, and stitch chandelier piece to silver twine. Folding napkin so edges are hidden, position ribbon at center, tie in the back, and snip off free ends.*

TEMPLATES

Use these templates for the projects found in Stockings and Tiny Presents, page 12; Turning Cards into Keepsakes, page 22; Ornaments and Everlasting Wreaths, page 34; Handmade Cards, page 106; and Favors for a Holiday Feast, 124. For the beaded snowflake, use the paper on which you photocopy the image as your template; to make the other templates, you'll need to trace the images onto kraft paper or thin cardboard.

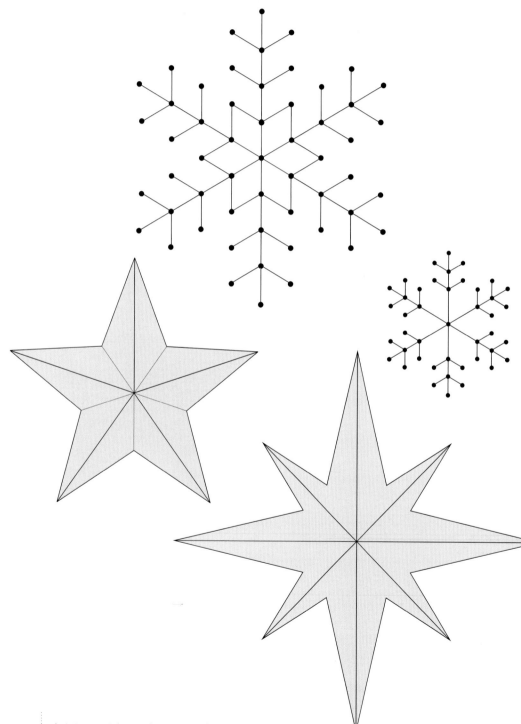

STARS AND SNOWFLAKES
Use the five-pointed star (far left) for the star above and on page 41. For the star below and on page 11, use the eight-pointed star (left). Photocopy the templates, enlarging to desired size. To make the beaded snowflakes on pages 12 and 13, photocopy the templates (above, left and far left), enlarging 125 percent.

STOCKINGS *To make the stockings above and on page 12, enlarge the large stocking template (far right) 225 percent on a photocopier. For the attached-cuff stockings on pages 15 and 21, you will also need the cuff template (above right), enlarged 225 percent. Use the small stocking template (below) to make the stocking cards on page 113 and the stocking place cards on page 126. Photocopy it, enlarging 150 percent or to desired size.*

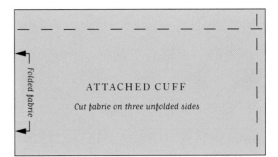

Folded fabric

ATTACHED CUFF
Cut fabric on three unfolded sides

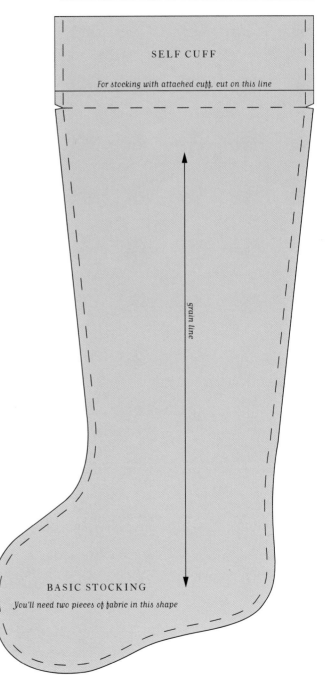

SELF CUFF

For stocking with attached cuff, cut on this line

grain line

BASIC STOCKING
You'll need two pieces of fabric in this shape

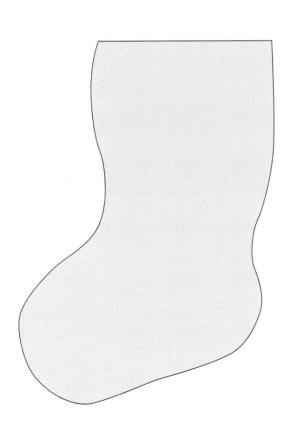

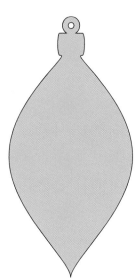

HOUSE OF CARDS *Use the measurements on the rectangle (below) to make a template for the House of Cards above and on page 22. Trace the template onto a piece of thin cardboard. Use a utility knife and a straightedge to cut precise slits in the sides of the cards for easy building.*

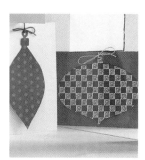

ORNAMENTS *For the ornament cards above and on page 113, use the pink templates (top, left and right). On a photocopier, enlarge them 150 percent or to desired size. Use the blue templates (right) to make the origami Christmas ornaments below and on page 42. Enlarge the templates 150 percent on a photocopier, or to desired size. Trace the templates onto thin cardboard or kraft paper, and cut out.*

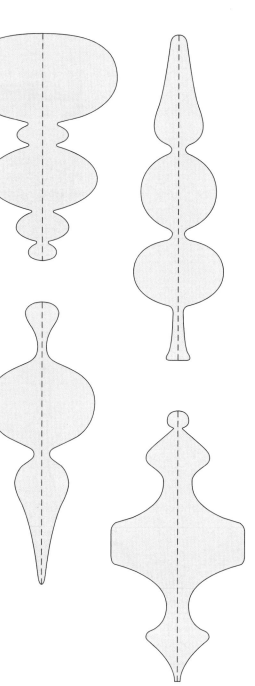

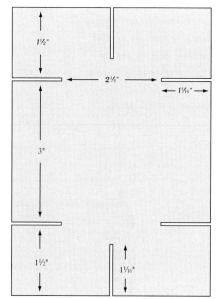

1½"

2⅛"

1¹⁄₁₆"

3"

1½"

1¹⁄₁₆"

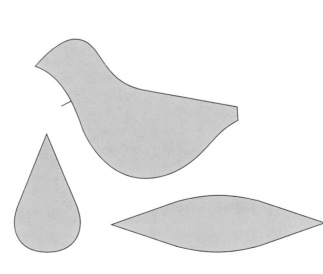

SNOWFLAKE AND
COCKTAIL GLASS *To
make the snowflake card
above and on page 113, use
the template (far left). Copy
template on a photocopier,
enlarging it to desired size.
Use the cocktail-glass template
(left), enlarged on a photocopier 125 percent, or to desired
size, to make the card below
and on page 113. Trace templates onto thin cardboard or
kraft paper, and cut out.*

FABRIC BIRD *To make
the fabric bird above and on
pages 34 and 35, use the
three pink templates (right)
for the bird's body, wing,
and breast. Enlarge the templates 200 percent, or to
desired size on a photocopier.
Trace the templates onto
thin cardboard or kraft
paper, and cut them out.*

THE GUIDE

Items pictured but not listed are from private collections. Addresses and telephone numbers of sources may change prior to or following publication, as may price and availability of any item.

COVER
Special thanks to Laura Surrey. SWEATER by TSE. PANTS by Loro Piana. SHOES by Hermès. GREENERY from US Evergreen, 805 Sixth Avenue, New York, NY 10001; 212-741-5300. 4" RED SATIN RIBBON from Hyman Hendler & Sons, 67 West 38th Street, New York, NY 10018; 212-840-8393. Minimum order $50. ARTIFICIAL APPLES from Pany Silk Flowers, 146 West 28th Street, New York, NY 10001; 212-645-9526.

page 2
GLASSES WITH ETCHED STARS (#3742), $348 for four, from Sentimento, 306 East 61st Street, New York, NY 10021; 212-750-3111. To the trade only. BACCARAT CHAMPAGNE GLASSES from Scully & Scully, 504 Park Avenue, New York, NY 10022; 212-755-2590. STERLING-SILVER FLATWARE from James Robinson, 480 Park Avenue, New York, NY 10022; 212-752-6166.

page 8
BENTO BOXES from Katagiri & Co., 224 East 59th Street, New York, NY 10022; 212-755-3566. 2" SATIN RIBBON and VELVET RIBBON from Hyman Hendler & Sons, 67 West 38th Street, New York, NY 10018; 212-840-8393. Minimum order $50. ANTIQUE GOLD and METALLIC RIBBONS and TASSELS from Tinsel Trading Co., 47 West 38th Street, New York, NY 10018; 212-730-1030. RED VENETIAN-GLASS VASE and PLATE and SEVENTEENTH-CENTURY MIRROR from Gardner & Barr, 213 East 60th Street, New York, NY 10022; 212-752-0555. FAUX-BAMBOO TABLE from Rooms & Gardens, 290 Lafayette Street, New York, NY 10012; 212-431-1297. WALL COLOR (#HC-76 FLAT) and TRIM (#HC-78 GLOSS) by Benjamin Moore, 800-826-2623 for local retailers.

STOCKINGS AND TINY PRESENTS

page 12
ASSORTED CASHMERE and WOOL-BLEND FABRICS, $40.95 to $82.95 per yard, from B & J Fabrics, 263 West 40th Street, New York, NY 10018; 212-354-8150. Minimum order 1/2 yard. 6MM (3815GB), 12MM (148GB), 25MM (1977GB), and 35MM SILVER-LINED CRYSTAL BUGLE BEADS (1192GB), $8 per 100 grams; and 6/0 SILVER-LINED CRYSTAL PONY BEAD (125GB), $7.50 per 100 grams, from Ornamental Resources,

P.O. Box 3010, Idaho Springs, CO 80452; 800-876-6762. Minimum order $25. 10/0 SILVER-LINED CRYSTAL ROCAILLE BEAD (STRUNG), $20 per kilogram, from Elliot, Greene & Company, 37 West 37th Street, New York, NY 10018; 212-391-9075.

page 15
TERRY CLOTH, $14.95 per yard, and WAFFLE WEAVE, $11.95 per yard, from Rosen & Chadick, 246 West 40th Street, New York, NY 10018; 212-869-0142. APOTHECARY GERANIUM LOTION, $12 per bottle, from Smith & Hawken, 394 West Broadway, New York, NY 10012; 800-776-3336. MILK NAIL POLISH, $12, ROSE TURKISH SOAP (oval), $8, JASMINE MILK SOAP (block), $10, and MUKKI EAU DE TOILETTE, $25, all from Fresh, 1061 Madison Avenue, New York, NY 10028; 212-396-0344. Q-TIPS, COTTON BALLS, POWDER PUFFS, and LOOFAH available at drug stores nationwide. LARGE ALUMINUM COMB, $15, COMPLEXION BRUSH, $22.50, BIO HAIRBRUSH, $18, and METAL SHOWER-CURTAIN CHAINS, $6.95, all from Ad Hoc Softwares, 410 West Broadway, New York, NY 10012; 212-925-2652. APOTHECARY JAR, $42, and NAIL BRUSH, $70, from Waterworks, 475 Broome Street, New York, NY 10013; 212-274-8800. R.R. TAN OILCLOTH, $9 per yard, M+M Industries, 450 Seventh Avenue, Suite 1203, New York, NY 10123; 212-239-9690. Minimum order 5 yards. ASSORTED FISHING FLIES; FISHING LINE, $6.50 for 2-pack of 15-foot leaders; WHEATLEY ALUMINUM FLY BOX (#1205-0053), $105; BATTENKILL 3/4" REEL (#1968-6100), $85; MALLARD DUCK SIDE FEATHERS, $2.10 per pack; WOOD DUCK FEATHERS, $5.50 per pack; and TYING THREAD, $1.50 per spool, from Orvis, 355 Madison Avenue, New York, NY 10017; 212-697-3133. CHOCOLATE SARDINES, $18, from Michael Boris Design, East and West Market Street, Rhinebeck, NY 12572; 914-876-5625. SINKERS, 50¢ to 95¢; JITTERBUG, $4.99; and CORK FLOATS, 2 for $2.99, from Capitol Fishing Tackle Company, 218 West 23rd Street, New York, NY 10011; 212-929-6132. COMPASS, $7, from Restoration Hardware, 935 Broadway, New York, NY 10010; 212-260-9479 or 800-

762-1005. CHARCOAL/KIWI/BORDEAUX #9 SOCKS, $28 per pair, Les Bas de Julie, C.P. 94, Saint-Irénée, Québec GOT 1VO; 800-650-3558. BRUSHES, $5.95 to $9.99, from Gracious Home, 1220 Third Avenue, New York, NY 10021; 212-517-6300, and from Top Service, 875 Seventh Avenue, New York, NY 10019; 212-765-3190. SHOELACES and SHOE POLISH from Top Service, see above. SHOE-POLISH APPLICATORS and PROPERT'S LEATHER AND SADDLE SOAP, from A & B Leather, 769 Tenth Avenue, New York, NY 10019; 212-265-8124. CHAMOIS, $2.99 per piece, The Art Store, 1—5 Bond Street, New York, NY 10012; 212-533-2444 or 888-546-2787 or www.artstores.com. NATURAL LINEN from Pearl Paint, 308 Canal Street, New York, NY 10013; 212-431-7932 or 800-221-6845. TERRA-COTTA POTS, $8 to $12, from AIX, 462 Broome Street, New York, NY 10013; 212-941-7919. VERDIGRIS-COPPER PLANT MARKER, $8; MINI PRUNERS, $32; BONSAI SHEARS, $48; and FROG, $5.95, from Smith & Hawken, 800-981-9888. JUTE TWINE, $2.59 per roll, from M & D Shapiro Hardware, 63 Bleecker Street, New York, NY 10012; 212-477-4180. SEED PACKETS from Shepherd's Garden Seeds, 30 Irene Street, Torrington, CT 06790; 800-255-0206. METAL GARDEN MARKER, $41.75 for 20 pieces, from Earthmade, 1502 Meridian Road, P.O. Box 609, Jasper, IN 47547; 800-843-1819. SHOOFLY BUG REPELLENT, $11.50; BAG BALM, $7.50; FARMER'S FRIEND HAND SALVE, $6.50; and HEDGE & ROW GARDEN GLOVES, $26, from Restoration Hardware, see above. RIBBONS from: Hyman Hendler & Sons, 67 West 38th Street, New York, NY 10018; 212-840-8393. Minimum order $50. M & J Trimmings, 1008 Sixth Avenue, New York, NY 10018; 212-391-9072.

page 16

BARKSDALE/TURF STRIPED LINEN (#91022-01), $59 per yard, from Rogers & Goffigon, 979 Third Avenue, Suite 1717, New York, NY 10022; 212-888-3242. To the trade only.

page 17

TEDDY-BEAR RATTLE (#7970), $14, from Bonpoint, 811 Madison Avenue, New York, NY 10021; 212-879-0900. CANDY CANE, $10.50 for set of 6, from Hammonds, 888-226-3999. YARN, $5.95 per roll, from The Yarn Connection, 218 Madison Avenue, New York, NY 10016; 212-684-5099.

page 20

LOUIS XVI-STYLE CHAISE LOUNGE CHAIR, $3,250, from Casita Antiques, 48 East 12th Street, New York, NY 10003; 212-253-1925. GRAY WOOL from B & J Fabrics, see above. STUFFED DOG, $8, from ABC Carpet & Home, 888 Broadway, New York, NY 10003; 212-473-3000. CANDY CANE, $10.50 for set of 6, from Hammonds, see above.

page 21

LOUIS XVI-STYLE DAYBED from Casita Antiques, see above. HANDKERCHIEF LINEN and WHITE COTTON DOTTED SWISS, both $24.95 per yard, from B & J Fabrics, see above.

page 22

ASSORTED CARDS, 60¢ each, from the Metropolitan Museum of Art, 800-662-3397. PASHMINA CASHMERE WRAP (ACW002), $359, from Martha By Mail; 800-950-7130 or www.marthabymail.com.

page 23

ASSORTED PAPER from New York Central Art Supply, 62 Third Avenue, New York, NY 10003; 800-950-6111. Minimum order $15.

page 24

GOLD-COVERED CHOCOLATE COINS, PORCELAIN BEADS WITH GREEN LETTERING, BASEBALL KEYCHAIN, and MINI COLORED PENCILS all from E.A.T. Gifts, 1062 Madison Avenue, New York, NY 10028; 212-861-2544.

page 26

SILVER TWINE, $1.75 per yard, from Tinsel Trading Co., 47 West 38th Street, New York, NY 10018; 212-730-1030. 1/4" CRAFT PUNCH from Family Treasures, 24922 Anza Drive, Unit A, Valencia, CA 91344; 800-413-2645.

page 27

BROWN and GOLD PAPER from New York Central Art Supply, see above. BLUE SKIER CARD from Crockett Cards, P.O. Box 1428, Manchester Center, VT 05255; 802-362-2913.

page 28

ICE-SKATE GIFT TAG from Stars & Eggplants, 27 West 20th Street, Suite 603, New York, NY 10011; 212-242-9942. NOEL CARD from Soolip Paperie & Press, 8646 Melrose Avenue, West Hollywood, CA 90069; 310-360-0545. EVERGREEN BOTANICAL CARD (#HS29) from B Designs, P.O. Box 1507, Haverhill, MA 01831; 978-374-3575. SILVER and VINTAGE RIBBON, BEADS, and TASSELS from Tinsel Trading Co., see above. BROWN MOUSE TAIL TRIM from M & J Trimmings, 1008 Sixth Avenue, New York, NY 10018; 212-391-9072.

page 29

GRAY WALL PAINT (#HC76) by Benjamin Moore, 800-826-2623 for local retailers. BROWN and GOLD RIBBON from Hyman Hendler & Sons, 67 West 38th Street, New York, NY 10018; 212-840-8393. Minimum order $50. NINETEENTH-CENTURY CHEST, $7,250, from Pierre Deux Antiques, 369 Bleecker Street, New York, NY 10014; 212-243-7740. WHITE CARD WITH TREE, "HAPPY HOLIDAYS" TREE CARD, CARD WITH TREE, CARD WITH CHURCH STEEPLE, and CARD WITH ANGELS from Claudia Laub Studio, 7404 Beverly Boulevard, Los Angeles, CA 90036; 323-931-1710. "VIRGIN OF THE ROSARY" CARD (#K9829A), "ANGEL WITH TRUMPET" CARD (#K9804A), and "FLIGHT INTO EGYPT" CARD (#K9422X), $3.95 each; GOLD WREATH CARD (#K9817A); and "ARCHANGEL GABRIEL" CARD (#K9702X), $10.95 for 10, from the Metropolitan Museum of Art, see above. DOVE CARD (#04998) from Papyrus, 800-872-7978. "NOEL" CARD from Soolip Paperie & Press, see above. GIFT TAGS from Stars & Eggplants, see above. "WELCOME CHRISTMAS"

REINDEER CARD and DOUBLE CORNUCOPIA CARD from Mrs. John L. Strong Fine Stationery, 699 Madison Avenue, New York, NY 10021; 212-838-3775. SNOWFLAKE CARD from Cathy Gigliotti, Ltd., 532 East Village Road, Suite B-1, Holland, PA 18966; 215-860-5170. CARD WITH WHEAT from William Arthur, 800-985-6581. CARD WITH PINECONE AND EVERGREEN BOTANICAL CARD (#HS29) from B Designs, see above. PURPLE CARD WITH SNOWFLAKES (#607) and DARK-GREEN CARD WITH ORNAMENTS (#604) from Lunalux Art and Design Workshop, 1618 Harmon Place, Minneapolis, MN 55403; 612-373-0526. CARD WITH URN from Studio Z Mendocino, 711 North Main Street, Fort Bragg, CA 95437; 707-964-9448. VIRGIN AND CHILD CARD (#67304) from Caspari, 800-227-7274. CARD WITH TREE AND ANIMALS, from William Arthur, see above. BLUE ORNAMENT CARD from Dempsey & Carroll, 110 East 57th Street, New York, NY 10022; 212-486-7526.

page 30

SMALL CARDS from Caspari, see above. SKATER GIFT ENCLOSURE, WHITE CARD WITH ACORN, WHITE CARD WITH ANGEL, MISTLETOE GIFT ENCLOSURE, and CARD WITH DEER AND HAPPY HOLIDAYS from B Designs, see above. "JOYEUX NOEL" CARD from Papyrus, see above. WHITE CARD WITH YELLOW SQUARE and SILVER STAR from Soolip Paperie & Press, see above. CARD WITH SNOWFLAKE and CARD WITH ICE SKATE from William Arthur, see above. CARD WITH WHITE LACE OVER WHITE PAPER from Cathy Gigliotti, see above. VINTAGE FRENCH SILVER RIBBON from Tinsel Trading Co., see above. ENGLISH SILVERPLATE CANDLESTICKS (#H2505), $845 per pair, and SILVERPLATE CLOCK (#J882) from Sentimento, 306 East 61st Street, New York, NY 10021; 212-750-3111. To the trade only.

page 31

GREEN SATIN RIBBON from Hyman Hendler & Sons, see above.

page 33

WALL PAINT (#1241) and TRIM (#1009) by Benjamin Moore, 800-826-2623 for local retailers. CARD WITH HOUSE and TREE from Julie Holcomb Printers, 1601 63rd Street, Emeryville, CA 94608; 510-654-6416. RED CARD WITH TREE and CARD WITH SLEIGH from Crockett Cards, see above. CARD WITH RED BALL and CARD WITH CIRCULAR PATTERN from B Designs, see above. GERMAN FLORAL GIFT CARDS (#K1911X), $4.95 for 8; "NOEL" CARD (#K9608X), $11.95 for 5; MADONNA CARD (#K9820X), $15.95 for 20; SNOWFLAKE CARD (#K9806K), $18.95 for 10; ROTHSCHILD MISELLARY CARD (#K0728), $15.95 for 8, all from the Metropolitan Museum of Art, see above. CARD WITH LACE STOCKING from Cathy Gigliotti, Ltd., see above. RED CARD WITH TREE and WHITE CARD WITH STAR PRINT from Claudia Laub Studio, see above. SMALL RED NOTE CARD (#02387) from Papyrus, see above. RED-AND-WHITE CARD WITH THREE KINGS, SANTA CARD, and X-MAS CARD from Stratford Antique Center, 400 Honeyspot Road, Stratford, CT 06615; 203-378-7754. RED CARD WITH GOLD ON FLAP, from Studio Z Mendocino, see above.

RED GIFT TAGS from Stars & Eggplants, see above.
WHITE CARD WITH RED CENTER AND GOLD HOLLY
from Mrs. John L. Strong Fine Stationery, see above.
MAHOGANY DESK WITH RED LEATHER TOP (#J688)
from Sentimento, see above. SILVER TRAY from
Maine Trading Company, 36 West 25th Street, New
York, NY 10010; 212-627-7195.

ORNAMENTS AND EVERLASTING WREATHS

page 34

ASSORTED FEATHERS from Cinderella Flowers, 48
West 37th Street, New York, NY 10018; 212-840-0644.
SILVER BEADS from Toho Shoji, 990 Sixth Avenue,
New York, NY 10018; 212-868-7465. Minimum order
$50. BIRD'S NEST from Bill's Flower Market, 816
Sixth Avenue, New York, NY 10001; 212-889-8154.

page 35

BENTWOOD OVAL BOX available at craft stores nationwide. ROSE WAX TISSUE PAPER from New York Central Art Supply, 62 Third Avenue, New York, NY
10003; 212-473-7705. Minimum order $15. 2 1/2"
FRENCH GROSGRAIN RIBBON, $7 per yard, from Hy-
man Hendler & Sons, 67 West 38th Street, New York,
NY 10018; 212-840-8393. Minimum order $50.

page 37

10" WREATH FORM, $2.49, from Bill's Flower Market,
see above. LIPSTICK-RED SEAM BINDING, $6.75 per
roll, from American Notions, 336 West 37th Street,
New York, NY 10018; 212-563-0480. 8MM RUBY DRUK
BEADS, $23 per mass (1,200 beads); and 10MM RUBY
DRUK BEADS, $42 per mass (1,200 beads), from Elliot,
Greene & Company, 37 West 37th Street, New York,
NY 10018; 212-391-9075. 6MM RED TRANSPARENT
DRUK BEADS, $22 per mass (1,200 beads), from Mayer
Imports, 25 West 37th Street, New York, NY 10018;
212-391-3830. 2" RED SATIN PICOT RIBBON, $6.75 per
yard, from Hyman Hendler & Sons, see above.

page 38

54"-WIDE RASPBERRY COTTON VELVET, $19.95 per
yard, from B & J Fabrics, 263 West 40th Street, New
York, NY 10018; 212-354-8150. Minimum order 1/2
yard. 5/8" FIRE-RED SOCIETY SATIN RIBBON, $4.50
per yard; 2" CERISE GROSGRAIN RIBBON, $5.75 per
yard; and ASSORTED RIBBONS, $2 to $18.50 per yard,
from Hyman Hendler & Sons, see above. ASSORTED
PAPER from New York Central Art Supply, see above.

page 41

LAMETTA ROPING from D. Blümchen & Co., 162 East
Ridgewood Avenue, P.O. Box 1210, Ridgewood, NJ
07451; 201-652-5595.

page 42

SILVER ORIGAMI PAPER, $4 for fifty 6" sheets, from
New York Central Art Supply, see above. SILVER
BEADS from Metalliferous, 34 West 46th Street, New
York, NY 10036; 212-944-0909. SILVER EMBROIDERY
FLOSS, $3 for 8.7 yards, from Stitches East, 55 East
52nd Street, New York, NY 10022; 212-421-0112.

page 43

JINGLE BELLS, 6 for $12, from Toho Shoji, see above.
16-GAUGE NICKEL WIRE, $15.35 per 1-pound spool;
and ROSARY PLIERS, $27.50, from Metalliferous, see
above. VINTAGE 4" SILVER-METAL RIBBON, $25 per
yard, from Tinsel Trading Co., 47 West 38th Street,
New York, NY 10018; 212-730-1030.

page 46

RECTANGULAR WOODEN BOX, $10, from Kate's
Paperie, 888-941-9169. 1 1/2", 6", and 10" RIBBON from
Tinsel Trading Co., see above.

page 47

LOUIS XVI SIDE CHAIRS, $5,500 for pair, from Pierre
Deux Antiques, 369 Bleecker Street, New York, NY
10014; 212-243-7740. ANTIQUE MIRRORED COFFEE
TABLE, $3,000, from Malmaison Antiques, 253 East
74th Street, New York, NY 10021; 212-288-7569.
ANTIQUE MURANO SCONCES, $3,900 per pair, from
Mercia Bross and John Salibello Antiques, 229 East
60th Street, New York, NY 10022; 212-688-7499.

SPECIAL GIFTS FOR ONE

page 50

RED RIBBON from Hyman Hendler & Sons, 67
West 38th Street, New York, NY 10018; 212-840-
8393. Minimum order $50. PLACEMENT BOX, $26;
SMALL ROUND BOX, $15; SMALL OVAL BOX, $12;
LARGE ROUND BOX, $19; and LARGE OVAL BOX, $19,
from Hofcraft, 800-828-0359.

page 53

GALVANIZED STEEL from Standard Tinsmith &
Roofer Supply, 183 Chrystie Street, New York,
NY 10002; 212-674-2240. GLASS VASE, $24, from
Global Table, 107—109 Sullivan Street, New York,
NY 10012; 212-431-5839. WOVEN STRAW BOX, $6,
from Ad Hoc Softwares, 410 West Broadway, New
York, NY 10012; 212-925-2652. 1/2" and 3/4" SPEC-
TRUM MAGNETS from Staples Office Supply Stores;
800-333-3330 for store locations. MARTHA STEWART
EVERYDAY GARDEN ENAMELS WATER-BASED
PRIMER and HIGH-GLOSS LATEX SPRAY PAINT in
"Loire Pink" from Kmart, 800-866-0086 for store
locations; also available from Sears mall stores, 800-
972-4687 for locations.

pages 54 and 55

FRENCH SILVER PAPER, $1 per sheet, from Papivore,
117 Perry Street, New York, NY 10014; 212-627-6055.
COLUMBIAN CERAMIC "CHAMBAWARE" BOWLS,
$8 to $12, from Be Seated, 66 Greenwich Avenue, New
York, NY 10011; 212-924-8444. Minimum order $15.
HEMLOCK BOWL, $30, from Dean & DeLuca, 560
Broadway, New York, NY 10021; 800-999-0306 or
www.dean-deluca.com. HANDMADE WOODEN BOWLS,
$9.25 to $43.75, from In the Woods, 9 Saint Marks
Place, New York, NY 10003; 212-673-1724. SMALL
STONEWARE BOWLS, $3.95 each, from H Store, 335
East 9th Street, New York, NY 10003; 212-477-2631.
WOODEN BOWLS, $5.89 to $9.65, from Hofcraft, see
above. ROSEWOOD BOWL, $70 to $150, from An
American Craftsman, 790 Seventh Avenue, New York,

NY 10019; 212-399-2555. SILVER RIBBONS, TRIM,
and THREADED BALLS, from Tinsel Trading Co., 47
West 38th Street, New York, NY 10018; 212-730-1030.
3/8" QUARTER-ROUND MOLDING, 23¢ per foot, from
Dykes Lumber Co., 348 West 44th Street, New York,
NY 10036; 212-246-6480. 3/32" BASSWOOD, $6.08 for
6"-by-24" sheet, from Pearl Paint, 308 Canal Street,
New Yo0rk, NY 10013; 212-431-7932 or 800-221-6845.
60-GRIT TURKISH EMERY GRAIN, $4.50 for 2 pounds,
from Global Product Systems, 103 East Taylor, P.O.
Box 605, Grant Park, IL 60940; 800-333-2833.

page 57

LINEN SOFA, $4,800, from Gomez Associates, 504
East 74th Street, New York, NY 10021; 212-288-6856.
NINETEENTH-CENTURY ENGLISH MAHOGANY
SIX-PANEL SCREEN, $7,500, from Amy Perlin
Antiques, 306 East 61st Street, New York, NY 10021;
212-593-5756.

page 58

MACHINE-EMBROIDERED MONOGRAMS by Penn &
Fletcher, 242 West 30th Street, 2nd Floor, New York,
NY 10001; 212-239-6868.

page 59

PURIST BOILED-WOOL CHILDREN'S SLIPPERS, $28,
from Garnet Hill, 800-622-6216.

page 60

8"-BY-10" FRAME, $9.50, from NY Central Framing,
212-420-6060. GOLDEN IRIDESCENT PEARL PAINT
and PAPER from New York Central Art Supply, see
above. PRESIDENTIAL BRAID, 79¢ per yard, from
M & J Trimmings, 1008 Sixth Avenue, New York, NY
10018; 212-391-9072. SASH PILLOWCASE, $70; FULL
FITTED SHEET, $175; and DUVET COVER, $315, from
Area; 212-924-7084 for retailer.

page 62 to 63

FIELDCREST CHARISMA STANDARD PILLOWCASE,
$60 for a pair; CHARISMA QUEEN SHEET, $90; QUEEN
SWIRL QUILT, $145; and STANDARD SWIRL QUILTED
SHAM, $35, from Garnet Hill, see above. NICKEL BAR
PULL and SATIN NICKEL HANDLE from Liz's Antique
Hardware, 453 South LaBrea, Los Angeles, CA 90036;
213-939-4403. WHITE-WASHED FRAME, $23, from
New York Central Art Supply, see above.

COOKIES AND CONFECTIONS

Page 64

ASSORTED BEADS from Toho Shoji, 990 Sixth
Avenue, New York, NY 10018; 212-868-7466.
Minimum order $50.

Pages 66 to 67

PEPPERMINT OIL, $4 per 1-ounce bottle, from
Dean & DeLuca, 560 Broadway, New York, NY
10021; 800-999-0306 or www.dean-deluca.com.
CANDY THERMOMETER, $17.95, and INSTANT-READ
THERMOMETER, $11.90, from Bridge Kitchenware,
214 East 52nd Street, New York, NY 10022; 212-838-
1901 or 800-274-3435 or www.bridgekitchenware.com.

Pages 69 to 70

MARZIPAN, $4.99 for 7 ounces, SPECTRUM SOFT GEL PASTE FOOD COLOR, $1.49 per 3/4-ounce bottle, and SUPERFINE SUGAR, $1.99 per 4-ounce container, from NY Cake & Baking Distributors, 56 West 22nd Street, New York, NY 10010; 212-675-2253 or 800-942-2539. FENNEL BRANCHES, $4.50 per 100-gram package, from Dean & DeLuca, see above.

Page 71

WECK JARS from Dean & DeLuca, see above. PAPER from New York Central Art Supply, 62 Third Avenue, New York, NY 10003; 212-477-0400. Minimum order $15. BREAD FLOUR, $3.25 per 5-pound bag, from King Arthur Flour Baker's Catalog, P.O. Box 876, Norwich, VT 05055; 800-827-6836 or www.kingarthurflour.com

Pages 72 to 76

ASSORTED RIBBON from: Hyman Hendler & Sons, 67 West 38th Street, New York, NY 10018; 212-840-8393. Minimum order $50. Tinsel Trading Co., 47 West 38th Street, New York, NY 10018; 212-730-1030. COLORED GLASSINE PAPER, 55¢ per sheet, and GREEN POLKA-DOT PAPER by Tamashiki, $4.40; RED-AND-WHITE PAPER by Bertini, $1.50 per sheet, from New York Central Art Supply, see above. FOOD-PACKAGING KIT (CKP001), $54, from Martha By Mail, 800-950-7130 or www.marthabymail.com.

Page 77

OFFSET SPATULA, $5.25 for 6 1/2" spatula, from Bridge Kitchenware, see above.

Page 78

CRANBERRY VENETIAN-GLASS PLATES and BOWL, from Gardner & Barr, 213 East 60th Street, New York, NY 10022; 212-752-0555. STERLING-SILVER FLATWARE from James Robinson, 480 Park Avenue, New York, NY 10022; 212-752-6166. CRYSTALLIZED GINGER, $10 per pound, and DRIED BLACK MISSION FIGS, $7 per pound, from Dean & DeLuca, see above. 2-CUP COLUMN MOLD WITH LID, $15.99, and 3-CUP FLUTED MOLD WITH LID, $15.99, from NY Cake & Baking Distributors, see above.

Pages 79

ASSORTED SATIN RIBBONS from Hyman Hendler & Sons, see above. TASSEL, SILVER-THREADED BEADS, and SILVER RIBBON and from Tinsel Trading Co., see above. FLOCKED PAPER from New York Central Art Supply, see above.

GIFTS FOR LONG, LONG LISTS

Page 80

CRACKLED WHITE CAFÉ AU LAIT BOWLS, $19, from Ad Hoc Softwares, 410 West Broadway, New York, NY 10012; 212-925-2652. RIBBON from Hyman Hendler & Sons, see above. PLACE CARDS from Kate's Paperie, 888-941-9169. IBARRA HOT CHOCOLATE, from Kitchen Market, 218 Eighth Avenue, New York, NY 10011; 212-243-4433.

Pages 82 to 83

ASSORTED RIBBONS from Hyman Hendler & Sons, see above.

Page 84

WOODGRAIN and WHITE WHITE CORRUGATED PAPER, ORANGE GIFT CARD AND ENVELOPE, GREEN VELLUM PAPER, and CORRUGATED CARDBOARD from Kate's Paperie, see above. ORANGE GROSGRAIN RIBBON (#255), YELLOW GROSGRAIN RIBBON (#225), GREEN GROSGRAIN RIBBON (#152), and BROWN VELVET RIBBON from Hyman Hendler & Sons, see above. SUGAR MOLDS (KBM001), $18, from Martha By Mail, 800-950-7130 or www.marthabymail.com. COTTAGE DELIGHT CITRUS PRESERVES from Foster's Market, 2694 Durham-Chapel Hill Boulevard, Durham, NC 27707; 919-489-3944, and from Myers of Keswick, 634 Hudson Street, New York, NY 10014; 212-691-4194. WOVEN BOX from Ad Hoc Softwares, see above. GOLD and PINK MINYEI PAPER SQUARE, $18.75, from New York Central Art Supply, 62 Third Avenue, New York, NY 10003; 212-473-7705. Minimum order $15.

Page 85

LUCO WHITE GLITTER, $2.74 for 4 ounces, from Pearl Paint, 308 Canal Street, New York, NY 10013; 212-431-7932 or 800-221-6845. PLASTIC TREES, 99¢ per pack, from NY Cake & Baking Distributors, see above. ANTIQUE MINIATURES, $3 and up, from Fun Antiques, 1101 First Avenue, New York, NY 10021; 212-838-0730. DURO QUICKSET EPOXY, $3.08 per pack, from The Art Store, 1—5 Bond Street, New York, NY 10012; 212-533-2444 or 888-546-2787 or www.artstores.com.

Page 88

ASSORTED SEASHELLS from Sanibel Seashell Industries, 905 Fitzhugh Street, Sanibel Island, FL 33957; 941-472-1603.

Page 89

DRIED HERBS, 35¢ to $1.60 per ounce, from Aphrodisia, 264 Bleecker Street, New York, NY 10014; 212-989-6440.

Page 90

ASSORTED RIBBONS from Hyman Hendler & Sons, see above. ANTIQUE SILVER BRAIDING and

SMALL ANTIQUE PINK BUTTONS, from Tinsel Trading Co., see above. ASSORTED BEADS from Toho Shoji, 990 Sixth Avenue, New York, NY 10018; 212-868-7466. Minimum order $50. LINEN-COVERED SKETCHBOOKS from New York Central Art Supply, see above.

Page 91

ASSORTED SUSAN SCHADT CANDLES, from Ad Hoc Softwares, see above; and from Covington Candle, 976 Lexington Avenue, New York, NY 10021; 212-472-1131. THIN NATURAL BEESWAX CANDLES from Zinc Details, 1905 Fillmore Street, San Francisco, CA 94115; 415-776-2100. LINEN PATTERNED GLASSINE PAPER, "TO" and "FROM" RUBBER STAMPS, and SILVER INK PADS, from Kate's Paperie, see above. SILVER RIBBON from Tinsel Trading Co., see above. ANTIQUE MIRROR, $750, from Gray Gardens, 461 Broome Street, New York, NY 10013; 212-966-7116.

SAVORIES FOR GIFTS AND GATHERINGS

page 92 to 93

BENTO BOXES from Katagiri & Co., 224 East 59th Street, New York, NY 10022; 212-755-3566. 2" SATIN and 1/2" VELVET CRIMSON RIBBONS from Hyman Hendler & Sons, 67 West 38th Street, New York, NY 10018; 212-840-8393. Minimum order $50. GOLD METALLIC RIBBONS and TASSELS from Tinsel Trading Co., 47 West 38th Street, New York, NY; 212-730-1030.

page 94

RED SATIN RIBBON from Hyman Hendler & Sons, see above. 1/4" GOLD METALLIC RIBBON from Tinsel Trading Co., see above. ROUND JARS WITH GASKETS from Williams-Sonoma, 800-541-2233.

page 95

ORGANZA FABRIC, RIBBON, and ANTIQUE GOLD BEADS from Tinsel Trading Co., see above. CANNING JARS, $.95 to $1.50, from Broadway Panhandler, 447 Broome Street, New York, NY 10013; 212-966-3434 or www. broadwaypanhandler.com. JAR LIFTER, $7.95; STAINLESS-STEEL TONGS, $3.95 to $5.95; and STAINLESS-STEEL CANNING FUNNEL, $17.95, from Bridge Kitchenware, 214 East 52nd Street, New York, NY 10022; 212-838-1901 or 800-274-3435 or www. bridgekitchenware.com. CANDIED ORANGE PEEL from Dean & DeLuca, 560 Broadway, New York, NY 10021; 800-999-0306 or www.dean-deluca.com.

page 96

MANDOLINE, $29.50, from Katagiri & Co., see above.

page 97

14" PASTRY BAG, $3.25; #2 TIP, $1.25; and 3/8" COUPLER, $1.25 for two, all from Broadway Panhandler, see above.

page 98

DOUBLE RECIPE BOX, $11.34, from Pearl Paint, 308 Canal Street, New York, NY 10013; 212-431-7932 or 800-221-6845. ANTIQUE YELLOW RIBBON, $5 and up, from Tinsel Trading Co., 47 West 38th Street, New York, NY 10018; 212-730-1030. 8"-BY-11" GOLD-BROCADE PAPER, $2.75 per sheet, and 21 1/2"-BY-31 1/2" MOKUBU PAPER (#006S), $4.05 per sheet, all from Kate's Paperie, 888-941-9169.

Page 99

1/4" RED VELVET and GREEN SATIN RIBBON from M & J Trimmings, 1008 Sixth Avenue, New York, NY 10018; 212-391-9072. EIGHTEENTH-CENTURY ENGRAVING, "THE OBSTINATE ONE," $1,650, from Pierre Deux, 369 Bleecker Street, New York, NY 10014; 212-243-7740. 2" ROSE SATIN RIBBON from Hyman Hendler & Sons, see above. 4-PLY WAXED LINEN TWINE from The Caning Shop, 926 Gilman Street, Berkeley, CA 94710; 510-527-5010. BAMBOO STEAMER, $18.95, from Kamman Food Products, 200 Canal Street, New York, NY 10013; 212-571-0330.

Page 100

RYE FLOUR, $1.95 per 2-pound bag, from King Arthur Flour Baker's Catalog, P.O. Box 876, Norwich, VT 05055; 800-827-6836 or www.kingarthurflour.com

Page 101

ANTIQUE SILVER THREADED BEAD, 3" ANTIQUE SILVER RIBBON, and 1/4" ANTIQUE SILVER RIBBON, from Tinsel Trading Co., see above. 9-CUP PANDORO MOLD, $30.95, from Bridge Kitchenware, see above.

HANDMADE CARDS
Special thanks to Steven Fraser of Masterstroke Canada.

page 106

ASSORTED PAPER from New York Central Art Supply, 62 Third Avenue, New York, NY 10003; 212-473-7705. Minimum order $15. MINIATURE RED-AND-WHITE GINGHAM RIBBON from Masterstroke Canada, 416-751-4193 or www.masterstrokecanada.com. WHITE FOLDED NOTE WITH RED BORDER from Crane's, 800-572-0024.

page 108

ASSORTED RIBBONS from Masterstroke Canada, see above. RUBBER STAMP SET, $39, from Tail of the

Yak, 2632 Ashby Avenue, Berkeley, CA 94705; 510-841-9891. DECORATIVE PAPERS from New York Central Art Supply, see above. 3/8" GROSGRAIN RIBBON, $1.50 per yard, from Bell'occhio, 8 Brady Street, San Francisco, CA 94103; 415-864-4048.

page 109

ASSORTED ENVELOPES from Kate's Paperie, 888-941-9169. FISKARS STAR-SHAPED PAPER PUNCH available at craft stores nationwide, or www.fiskars.com for information.

page 110

PFAFF "CREATIVE" 7550 SEWING MACHINE from Pfaff American Sales Corp., 610 Winters Avenue, Paramus, NJ 07652; 201-262-7211.

page 111

STRIPED RIBBON from Hyman Hendler & Sons, 67 West 38th Street, New York, NY 10018; 212-840-8393. Minimum order $50. GINGHAM RIBBON from Bell'occhio, see above. ASSORTED GLASSINE ENVELOPES from American Printing & Envelope Company, 900 Broadway, 4th Floor, New York, NY 10003; 212-475-1204 or 800-221-9403.

page 112 to 113

SNOWFLAKE TEMPLATES from *Ready-To-Use Snowflake Designs* by Mack Fraga (Dover Publications, 1991; $5.95); 516-294-7000. FISKARS SOFT-TOUCH MICROTIP SCISSORS available at craft stores nationwide. WAXED-LINEN THREAD, $8.50 for 100 yards, from The Caning Shop, 926 Gilman Street, Berkeley, CA 94710; 510-527-5010. STRIPED RIBBON from Hyman Hendler & Sons, see above. GINGHAM RIBBON, $3 per yard, from Bell'occhio, see above. DECORATIVE PAPERS from New York Central Art Supply, see above. ASSORTED GLASSINE ENVELOPES from American Printing & Envelope Company, see above.

WRAPS, TAGS, BUNDLES, AND BOWS

Page 114

3' TINSEL TREE (XTT001), $198, and EMBOSSED WRAPPING PAPER (CMM006), $18 per roll, from Martha By Mail; 800-950-7130 or www.marthabymail.com. ASSORTED PAPER from New York Central Art Supply, 62 Third Avenue, New York, NY 10003; 212-473-7705. Minimum order $15. ASSORTED RIBBON from Hyman Hendler & Sons, 67 West 38th Street, New York, NY 10018; 212-840-8393. Minimum order $50.

Page 117

PAPER FOR PINWHEELS from New York Central Art Supply, see above. MAP PINS from Hagstrom Map and Travel Center, 57 West 43rd Street, New York, NY 10036; 212-398-1222. 6MM CLEAR DRUK BEAD available from craft stores nationwide. EMBOSSED WRAPPING PAPER (CMM006), $18 per roll, from Martha By Mail, see above.

Pages 118 to 119

WRAPPING PAPERS available from: Kate's Paperie, 888-941-9169. New York Central Art Supply, see above. Paper Access, 23 West 18th Street, New York, NY 10011; 212-463-7035. RIBBON available from: Hyman

Hendler & Sons, see above. Kate's Paperie, see above. RUG from ABC Carpet & Home, 888 Broadway, New York, NY 10003; 212-473-3000. CHAIRS, SIDE TABLE, and THROW PILLOW from Gomez Associates, 504 East 74th Street, New York, NY 10021; 212-288-6856.

Page 120

RED-AND-ORANGE INDIAN-BLOCK-PRINT PAPER, $3 to $3.80 per 20"-by-28" sheet, from New York Central Art Supply, see above.

FAVORS FOR A HOLIDAY FEAST

Page 124

ANTIQUE SILVER RIBBON and SILVER THREAD from Tinsel Trading Co., 47 West 38th Street, New York, NY 10018; 212-730-1030.

Page 126

PAPER from New York Central Art Supply, 62 Third Avenue, New York, NY 10003; 212-473-7705. Minimum order $15. 4-PLY WAXED LINEN TWINE from The Caning Shop, 926 Gilman Street, Berkeley, CA 94710; 510-527-5010.

Page 127

ANISE EXTRACT, $4 per 1-ounce bottle, from Dean & DeLuca, 560 Broadway, New York, NY 10021; 800-999-0306 or www.dean-deluca.com. FOUR-WREATHS MOLD (#5422), $49.50, from The-House-on-the-Hill, P.O. Box 7003, Villa Park, IL 60180; 630-969-2624 or www.houseonthehill.net. Catalog $2. SQUARE FLUTED COOKIE CUTTER SET, $15, and ALPHABET COOKIE CUTTER SET, $35, from Bridge Kitchenware, 214 East 52nd Street, New York, NY 10022; 212-838-1901 or 800-274-3435 or www.bridgekitchenware.com. SANDING SUGAR, $1.99 per 4-ounce package, and LUSTER and PEARL DUSTS, each $3.00 for 2 grams, from NY Cake & Baking Distributors, 56 West 22nd Street, New York, NY 10010; 212-675-2253 or 800-942-2539. SANDING SUGAR SET (KSS001), $38, from Martha By Mail; 800-950-7130 or www.marthabymail.com.

Page 129

STERLING-SILVER FLATWARE "IRISH RIB" from James Robinson, 480 Park Avenue, New York, NY 10022; 212-752-6166. 1/4" SILVER METALLIC THREAD from Tinsel Trading Co., see above.

Page 130

DECANTER WITH STERLING-SILVER NECK and HANDLE, $1,500, and GLASSES WITH ETCHED STARS, $348 for set of 4, from Sentimento, 306 East 61st Street, New York, NY 10021; 212-750-3111. To the trade only. BACCARAT CHAMPAGNE GLASSES from Scully & Scully, 504 Park Avenue, New York, NY 10022; 212-755-2590. STERLING-SILVER FLATWARE "ENGLISH THREAD" PATTERN from James Robinson, see above. WINE RINSERS from L. Becker Flowers, 217 East 83rd Street, New York, NY 10028; 212-439-6001.

CONTRIBUTORS

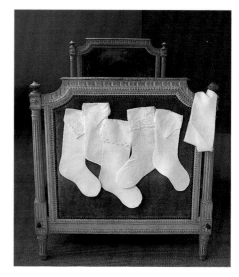

Creating a book as magical as this one requires the time and energy of a great many people. Special thanks to design director Eric A. Pike, whose passion for Christmas is evident on every page and to Annie Block, who worked tirelessly to perfect the text. Thank you, too, to the editors, art directors, and stylists whose inspirational ideas contributed to the creation of this volume, notably Gia Russo Adams, Stephana Bottom, Esther Bridavsky, Kerin Brooks, Claudia Bruno, Anthony Cochran, James Dunlinson, Stephen Earle, Agnethe Glatved, Lisa Hammerquist, Toby Hanson, Julie Hoffer, Lilian Hough, Joelle Hoverson, Jocelyn Joson, Fritz Karch, Megen Lee, Jodi Levine, Judith Lockhart, Peter Mars, Sophie Mathaulin, Hannah Milman, Pamela Morris, Sara Neumeier, Page Marchese Norman, Laura Normandin, Ayesha Patel, Claire Perez, Helen Quinn, Jennifer Scappatura, Claudia Schwartz, Scot Schy, Wendy Sidewater, Susan Spungen, Duane Stapp, Laura Surrey, Gael Towey, Gregory Wegweiser, and Lenore Welby; and to everyone at Oxmoor House, Clarkson Potter, Satellite Graphics, and Quebecor Printing. Finally, thank you to Martha, for inspiring us to reach for the best.

PHOTOGRAPHY

Bill Abranowicz
front covers, page 18

Christopher Baker
back cover, pages 3, 4, 6, 7 (center), 10, 11, 48, 49, 58, 59, 60 (right), 61 (top left, bottom row), 104, 105

Anita Calero
pages 7 (bottom), 15, 17 (right), 20, 21, 60 (left), 61 (center row), 106, 108, 109, 110 (top, bottom left, bottom center), 111-113, 136, 142

Dana Gallagher
pages 22, 27 (top), 28 (bottom), 29, 30, 31 (bottom left, right), 32-35, 38 (left), 137

Gentl & Hyers
pages 2, 9, 16, 24, 26, 27 (bottom right), 38 (right), 43, 45 (top), 46 (top), 56, 57, 62, 63, 66, 67, 69, 70, 80, 82-85, 86 (bottom right), 88-93, 99 (top left, bottom left), 124, 126, 128 (right), 129-131, 140, 143

Stephen Lewis
pages 42, 44 (top), 50, 53, 54 (left), 55 (top row, bottom left)

Victoria Pearson
pages 41, 47, 122, 123

Maria Robledo
pages 68, 71, 98, 99 (top right), 103

David Sawyer
page 99 (bottom right)

Victor Schrager
page 64

Matthew Septimus
pages 17 (left) 27 (bottom left), 39, 44 (bottom row), 45 (bottom row), 46 (bottom row), 86 (top row, bottom left), 87, 96, 97, 100, 110 (bottom right), 127, 128 (left)

Tara Sgroi
pages 5, 118, 119, 141

Luca Trovato
page 120

Anna Williams
pages 8, 54 (right), 55 (bottom center left, bottom center right, bottom right), 72-76, 78, 79, 94, 95, 101

Simon Watson
pages 7 (top), 12, 13, 23, 25, 28 (top), 31 (top), 37, 114, 115, 117

ILLUSTRATIONS

Harry Bates
pages 16, 18, 19, 40, 56, 121

If you have enjoyed this book, please join us as a subscriber to MARTHA STEWART LIVING *magazine. The annual subscription rate is $26 for ten issues. Call toll-free 800-999-6518, or visit our Web site. www.marthastewart.com.*

INDEX